ORACLE BONES, STARS, AND WHEELBARROWS

ORACLE BONES, STARS, AND WHEELBARROWS

Ancient Chinese Science and Technology

FRANK ROSS, Jr.

Illustrated by Michael Goodman

Houghton Mifflin Company   Boston   1982

The author extends warm thanks to Doris Hannigan
for typing this manuscript.

Library of Congress Cataloging in Publication Data

Ross, Frank Xavier, 1914-
    Oracle bones, stars, and wheelbarrows.

    Bibliography: p.
    Includes index.
    Summary: Discusses the achievements of the ancient
Chinese in astronomy, medicine, science, and engineering,
as well as such influential Chinese inventions as paper,
printing, gunpowder, and the compass.
    1. Science—China—History—Juvenile literature.
2. Engineering—China—History—Juvenile literature.
[1. Science—China—History.   2. Technology—China—History.   3. Inventions—China—History.   4. China—Civili-
zation]   I. Goodman, Michael,   II. Title.
Q127.C5R67   509.31   81-20137
ISBN 0-395-32083-6   AACR2

Printed in the United States of America

V 10 9 8 7 6 5 4 3 2 1

To E. A. Bonfils-Roberts, M.D., F.A.C.S., F.A.C.C.
In Deepest Gratitude

Contents

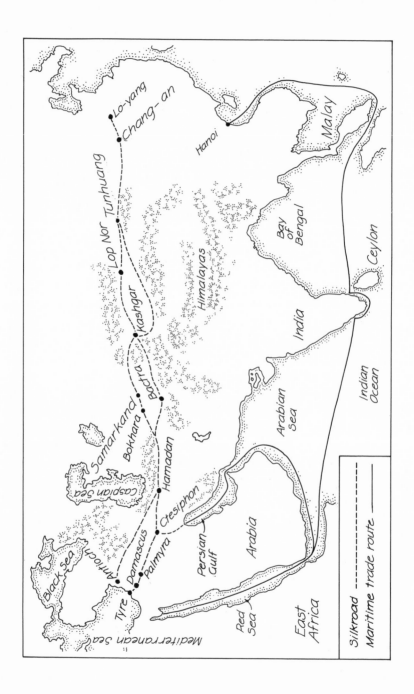

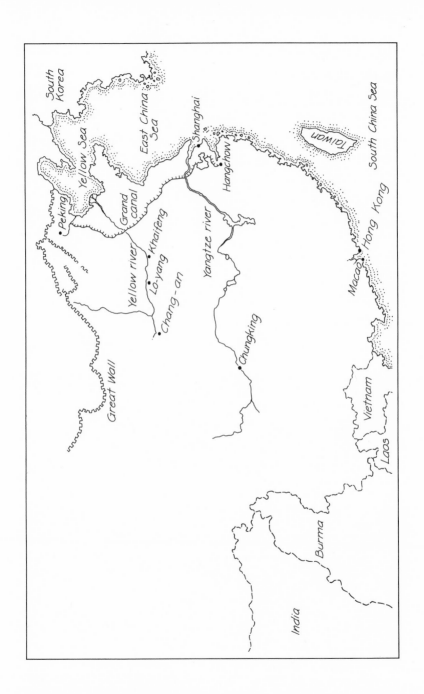

ORACLE BONES, STARS, AND WHEELBARROWS

Introduction

The West long believed that ancient China achieved little of importance in the fields of science and technology. There were a number of reasons for this attitude, which existed right up to the early decades of our own century. China's remoteness from the West was one of the more important. Although China is a huge land — about the size of the United States — there was a vast distance between the Eastern and Western worlds. Further, rugged mountains and enormous expanses of desert fill this stretch of the earth's surface, offering little encouragement for traveling across the region.

This is not to say that efforts to establish land connections between China and the West were not made. In all likelihood, they were. After all, we must assume that there were individuals in ancient times who, like those of later ages, were curious about the lands beyond their immediate world. But we can also assume that these attempts in antiquity were few and far between. After the dawn of the Christian era they became more numerous and permanent. There will be more said on this subject in the final chapter of the book.

Another barrier that hindered the West's knowledge about China was the language of that country. In ancient times, as now, the Chinese language was basically ideographic in nature: ideas are expressed with pictographic symbols. These are extremely simplified drawings of such objects as a tree, a mountain, the stars, and, indeed, everything seen and used in the world of the Chinese. The idea of shooting an arrow, for example, would be depicted by the highly stylized symbol of an arrow across a drawn bow.

As the Chinese language evolved, newer symbols were added whose meanings were quite complex. This made matters extremely difficult for Western scholars, who, in their attempts at interpreting the language, often arrived at different meanings for the various symbols. Consequently, the translations of Chinese writings in general, and science and technology in particular, frequently produced little more than confusion.

It was not until the studies of modern scholars, especially since the early decades of the twentieth century, that the truly remarkable attainments of scientists and technologists in ancient China became clear to the West. These new studies have shown that in a number of instances the Chinese scientists were the equal of — and, more often than not, superior to — their counterparts in the Western world. In astronomy and mathematics, for example, they had advanced the frontiers of knowledge that Western scientists were not to attain until centuries later.

As for ancient Chinese technical achievements, it has been said that just four of their inventions — paper-making, printing, gunpowder, and the magnetic compass — have influenced human affairs throughout the world as have no other of man's technical triumphs.

Throughout this book the traditional (Wade-Giles) spelling of names has been followed rather than the modern style, since this form is still more familiar to most westerners. Bear in mind that the Chinese language permits the same name to be spelled several different ways. It should also be noted that there is frequent use of qualified dates. This is particularly true for events that took place before 841 B. C. It must be remembered that the happenings occurred a long time ago, and whatever efforts may have been made to record them have long since disappeared.

Scholars have thus been forced to work with little surviving evidence. And even this has often proved hopelessly confusing or has had tantalizingly scarce detail. As a result, scholars have often found it necessary to substitute an approximation of the time of an event. Matters improved in the centuries following the birth of Christianity, when written accounts became more numerous and more durable, and historians were able to conduct their studies on a more factual basis. They were also helped by archaeological findings that told them much about the civilization of the ancient Chinese. As additional old written records are found and studied and new discoveries made in archaeological "digs," more precise dating of past events may well become possible.

Although the West had long been unaware of the accomplishments of Chinese scientists and technologists of antiquity, this attitude has changed drastically in modern times. As more scholarly studies are completed, there is a growing admiration for the originality and far-reaching influence of their work. This feeling should be shared by anyone who reads a book, writes on notepaper, or watches the launching of a rocket-powered spacecraft on the TV screen. All have a heritage reaching back to ancient China.

1. Astronomy

People have looked up at the stars since time beyond remembrance. The beauty and mystery of celestial phenomena have long held us in awe and wonder. Enthralled, yet lacking in understanding of heaven's spectacular displays, many peoples of ancient times incorporated the cosmos into their religious beliefs. The universe became for them the dwelling place of powerful spirits who profoundly affected the real world and its inhabitants. This concept was nowhere stronger than among the Chinese.

Ancient Chinese kings and emperors were surrounded by royal advisers, an elite group. Among the more important of these were scholars who observed and studied the stars. It was their responsibility to record the movement of the stars, phases of the moon, eclipses, and the appearances of comets. These astronomical events had then to be interpreted as messages from the heavenly spirits. Today these scholars would be known as astrologers. A ruler would make no move — start a military campaign, construct a palace, or even lay out the boundaries for a new city in his realm — without first consulting his astrologers.

When a new king ascended the throne, one of his first acts was to call in the chief astrologer and order the creation of a new calendar or the revision of the old one. The calendar represented a kind of physical link between the spirits of the universe and the real world. It told of such future happenings as the start of the monsoon season, the time of the spring thaw, drought, floods, and an eclipse of the moon. It was much like a present-day almanac. The ancient Chinese were an agricultural people, as they largely are today. Often nature, or the spirits, would strike them with disastrous droughts or floods. These happenings, critical in the lives of the people, supposedly were foretold by the calendar. If they were not, unrest developed among the king's subjects.

It was extremely important, therefore, that the chief astrologer and his assistants read the stars correctly. If they scored poorly with their predictions, it was the king who bore the wrath of the peasants. When disasters or other unpleasant events struck, the people believed that their ruler was no longer in the good graces of the heavenly spirits. Consequently, they no longer felt duty-bound to be loyal to their monarch.

Much the same feeling of disenchantment would be felt by the members of the royal court. From the king's standpoint this was even more dangerous than the lack of support of the people. Now he could expect all sorts of plots to remove his crown and possibly his head. Since a king's reign depended so much on the accuracy of the astrologers' work, these specialists had to know their profession. Too many failures could mean a sudden ending to their careers and lives.

Although the ancient Chinese scholars who devoted their studies to the stars were primarily astrologers, their labors did take them into areas of what we understand as the science of astronomy. In that sense they were pioneer astronomers, and very good ones. They were on a par with, and in many instances more advanced than, those of other lands — Babylonians, Egyptians, Greeks, and even the ancient astronomers of the New World, the Aztecs and Mayas. Indeed, as will be seen presently, some of their astronomical accomplishments have endured to the present day.

But a word or two more about astrology. In time, after the introduction of formal religions, like Buddhism, Taoism, and Christianity, astrology became less important among the Chinese. However, belief in the power of the stars to influence lives and events was never completely abandoned. It flourishes even today. And, as we know, astrology is not confined to China. This faith in the stars is of interest throughout the world. In the United States countless thousands of people would never dream of making a major move affecting their lives without first consulting the stars.

Archaeological evidence, in the form of oracle bones — one of the earliest and most primitive means ancient Chinese used for their written records — tells

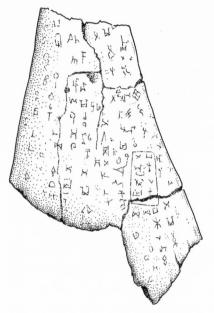

Oracle bones give evidence of earliest Chinese science

us that the Chinese astronomers were busily scanning the heavens fourteen centuries before the advent of Christianity. This long-buried evidence gives us records of solar and lunar eclipses, and other celestrial phenomena. And legend has it that eclipses were being noted as far back as 3000 and 2000 B.C. It is clear, from whatever source we use for our information, that these scientists were at their specialized tasks for a long time indeed.

Chinese astronomers of antiquity covered an astonishing range of astronomical features. Eclipses of the sun and moon, sunspots, comets, novas, supernovas, and the precise locations of the more prominent stars may read like a listing of the study areas of modern-day astronomers. Surprisingly enough, these were all of considerable interest to ancient Chinese sky observers. The records they left of their sightings, many from the earliest times, were remarkable for their accuracy. The fact that they carried on their studies with the naked eye, in contrast to the highly sophisticated apparatus astronomers use today, makes their achievements all the more outstanding.

Among the earliest, and surely more outstanding, accomplishments of the Chinese astronomers was their ability to select major stars in the heavens and measure their locations with mathematical accuracy. In order to do this they devised an equatorial coordinate system of measurement. Stars were positioned on circles measured in degrees from the equator, which served as a base line.

Of help to the astronomers in performing this task was a very old astronomical instrument, the armillary sphere. The device was one of the few at their disposal. The instrument, generally made of bronze, was a metal sphere composed of a series of intersecting scaled circles. The armillary was a physical model of the universe as conceived by the ancient astronomers, a kind of spherical shroud, or dome, enveloping the earth. The shroud was also of infinite distance from the earth. Stars whose positions on the shroud were to be measured were located on the rings of the armillary. The rings, as we have seen, were not parallel, but intersected one another. All the rings were scaled from a base ring, which represented the equator.

We do not know where the armillary sphere originated. The Chinese may have created it, although they were certainly not the sole users of the instrument. The armillary was also employed by astronomers of the Mediterranean region. Greek astronomers used the armillary to great advantage in their studies of the stars. They too were excellent astronomers of ancient times, and for centuries the science of astronomy in the West was based on knowledge acquired by Greek astronomers. The spherical armillary used by Greek scientists differed from the Chinese version. The base measuring ring on the Greek instrument represented the apparent path of the earth through the stars. The Greek star-measuring method became known as the ecliptic system.

Later, following the Greek civilization, the Arabs also made use of the armillary sphere. Enthusiastic astronomers, they devised still a third method for measuring the location of the stars. Theirs became known as the altazimuth. With this, star positions were plotted on an arc segment of the curving horizon line.

The most modern of the star-measuring methods is the galactic coordinate system. This involves the use of a complex computerized navigation system spewing out numbers while locked in on a galaxy, such as the Milky Way.

To return to the world of Chinese antiquity, Shih Shen and Kan Tê, scholars who were deeply interested in astronomy, prepared a star chart in approximately 350 B.C. They selected and located some eight hundred of the heavenly bodies. Their chart is considered the earliest of such astronomical records in which degrees were used to measure the positions of the stars. In order to accomplish their feat, the Chinese astronomers would have had to employ an instrument of some sort, namely, the armillary sphere. If historical evidence one day should prove this to be so, then the background of that instrument is even older than we now know it to be.

The oldest star chart in the West known at present has been attributed to the Greek astronomer Hipparchus (190–125 B.C.). A renowned scientist of the ancient world, Hipparchus based his star measurements on the ecliptic system.

Since the time of Shih Shen and Kan Tê, Chinese astronomers found the task of locating stars of particular interest. Numerous other astronomers, like Lohsia Hung (circa 100 B.C.) and Chang Hêng (A.D. 78–139), who also acquired considerable renown, followed in the path of the two pioneers. Fixing the positions of stars was really incidental to their main task of making new calendars or correcting an old one.

Kaifeng, in Honan Province, was a bustling capital city during the Sung Dynasty (960–1279). Its streets were a moving current of people: peasants bringing their farm produce to market; colorfully robed officials from the outlying provinces and their servants on their way to pay respects to the emperor or to consult with government officials; squads of soldiers, their lances glistening in the sunlight, marching to one of the gates of the walled city heading for a frontier outpost; and a crowd of grownups and children in a corner of the public square being amused by a troupe of traveling jugglers and acrobats.

At the end of the capital city was another walled compound. By contrast with the city itself, all was peaceful, almost serene, within the enclave. There was no wonder at this since within the walled area was the palace of the emperor. Besides his official residence there were nearby government buildings and the homes of members of the royal court. Removed from all the other structures, in a remote part of the walled compound, was the official observatory. Here the chief astronomer and his staff recorded their observations of the previous night, worked on star charts, and kept the calendar as up to date as possible.

The scientific nature of the building was clearly shown by an armillary sphere and gnomon mounted on the nearby grounds. The gnomon was another of the instruments frequently used by astronomers of ancient times. Its purpose was to measure the passage of time. As the sun shone upon the gnomon at various periods of the day, the length of the shadow cast would be gauged and the time calculated.

But the armillary sphere was by far the more noteworthy of the two instruments. The one erected on the grounds of the Kaifeng Observatory in 1088 had been made by a brilliant scientist, Su Sung. When his crea-

The armillary sphere was a model of the universe

tion was completed and installed at the observatory, no other in all the empire could equal it.

Tireless in his work, Su Sung nevertheless found the time to write an exhaustive account of his armillary sphere with its clockwork drive. The book contained many illustrations.

One of the features that made Su's armillary the finest of its time was the clock-driven mechanism, which enabled the instrument to operate almost automatically. This feature also gave the instrument some historical fame, since scholars of Chinese scientific and technical accomplishments say it was the first instrument for astronomical observation purposes to be equipped with such a mechanical device. The viewing telescopes of today have similar electrically driven mechanisms to enable them to follow automatically a star as it moves in the sky.

The great Kaifeng Observatory became renowned throughout the empire not only for the superlative instruments with which it was equipped, but also because of the important work performed there by Su Sung and his assistants. As chief astronomer, he had been requested to prepare new star charts. Many new events had been observed in the heavens since the previous charts were made, and they were now considered outdated. Over a period of six years, Su Sung and his scholarly assistants worked long and carefully to complete five star charts.

Because paper and printing were now in existence, the chief astronomer and his staff could prepare as many printed copies of these charts as the emperor might want. Previously, copies had to be made by the slow and tedious hand method. Su's printed copies of star charts are considered a pioneer development, one that the western world had to wait several centuries to duplicate.

Su Sung's work with armillary spheres and star

charts created ripples in astronomy that lasted more than five centuries. The Chinese astronomer's work was to have particular significance for Tycho Brahe (1546–1601), a celebrated Danish astronomer. He followed closely on the heels of the great Polish astronomer Copernicus (1473–1543), who startled the scientists and clergy of his day with the revolutionary theory that the earth revolved around the sun. Thus, the Greek concept of the sun moving around the earth that existed for more than fifteen centuries was thrown overboard.

Tycho Brahe's role in astronomy was primarily that of an observer — a very good one, as he proved during

An ancient star chart

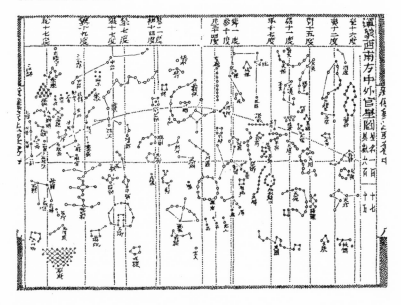

two decades of studying the night skies. Financially supported, and encouraged by King Frederick II, Brahe built the finest observatory in all of Europe. He constructed his sky-viewing station on the Island of Hveen and called it Uraniborg. Here, in a quiet setting, favored often by black-velvet night skies with stars of crackling brilliance, he and his assistants worked patiently, viewing, recording, and positioning the celestial bodies on charts. These superb star charts, the most accurate and complete ever compiled by an astronomer, became Tycho Brahe's legacy to the science of astronomy. Indeed, because of the charts' completeness and accuracy Brahe is often referred to as the father of observational astronomy.

Two of Tycho Brahe's major achievements in astronomy had a remarkable similarity to those of the ancient Chinese astronomers. The first was the large armillary sphere he erected at Uraniborg. Positioned in such a way that the equator served as a base line for determining star locations, it employed the equatorial mounting that the Chinese had devised for their armillaries more than five centuries earlier.

The second of Tycho Brahe's outstanding accomplishments was his method of making star charts. He measured the positions of the celestial bodies on the basis of the equatorial-coordinate system. Here again ancient Chinese astronomers had anticipated the Danish astronomer's work by more than a thousand years. This star-measuring method, introduced to Western observers by Brahe, has ever since been used by astronomers.

Had Brahe learned of these two outstanding Chinese contributions to astronomy? Did he somehow come into possession of a copy of a Chinese star chart? Was it through a translated Arabic account of these Chinese achievements? Or did he achieve these astronomical advances independently? Throughout the history of science and technology the independent occurrences of a scientific discovery or invention in widely separated parts of the world have happened frequently. Modern scholars have so far been unable to pin down definitely any of these possibilities.

Whether or not the Danish astronomer acquired his information from the writings of Chinese astronomers, Brahe's introduction and use of some of these important features, like the equatorial-coordinate system, did much to advance the science as it existed in the West in the sixteenth century. It is a measure of the quality of the work performed by the ancient Chinese astronomers that their star-positioning system and means for making star charts endure to this day. When American astronauts voyaged through space en route to the moon, the ancient Chinese equatorial-coordinate method for the positioning of stars was a key element in their system of navigation.

The sun pours out its energy with a blinding brilliance. Indeed, the intensity of its brightness is such that it can permanently injure one's vision if one looks at it directly for even a very short time. Despite this hazard and the lack of adequate instruments, Chinese astronomers managed to study the sun. They were probably the first to see and report sunspots.

Chinese astronomers' earliest record of sunspots dates from 28 B.C. From that time until the early seventeenth century they left accounts of sighting 112 such solar phenomena. Describing what they had seen, the astronomers noted the size of the sunspots and compared them to such earthly things as coins or hens' eggs.

European astronomers lagged far behind their Chinese counterparts when it came to observing and reporting sunspots. For more than sixteen centuries, Western astronomers had little or nothing to say about solar blemishes.

Perhaps the church's dogmatic attitude was responsible for this long period of ignorance. For centuries the church controlled intellectual activity in Europe. New concepts, like those in science, were generally condemned and their originators punished. Not until Galileo Galilei (1564–1642) had perfected his telescope and aimed it at the sun in 1610 did a European scientist take note of the phenomenon of sunspots. Defying church authorities, at great personal risk, Galileo published his findings three years later, along with other unorthodox scientific beliefs. In part, this is what the Renaissance astronomer reported: ". . . in the face of the sun itself, by the help of the telescope, certain dense and obscure substances . . . very like to the fogs about the earth are seen to be produced and dissolved."

The European Renaissance, from about the fourteenth century through the sixteenth, marked a dramatic change from medieval to more modern, enlightened thought. It was a period of brilliant, unrestrained intellectual achievement in literature, art, and science. Astronomy, along with other branches of the science, made impressive advances. It was out of this intellectual upheaval that eventually, by the nineteenth century, astronomers in Europe were able to explain in good measure the correct nature of sunspots.

Briefly, these were described as enormous clouds producing intense magnetic radiation. The clouds contract and expand in eleven-year cycles. Twentieth-century astronomers found that when sunspots are at their greatest, their magnetic radiation disturbs the planet Earth in a number of ways. Most important perhaps is the effect on radio transmission, which at times may be completely blacked out.

Novas are dim stars that suddenly increase in brightness and then, in a day or a week, disappear. Supernovas do much the same, but with an extraordinary brilliance. What happens is that the stars undergo explosions of tremendous dimensions and are transformed from celestial bodies to cosmic dust. Supernovas, the really spectacular performers, are relatively rare. Astronomers can expect to see these about once every century.

Despite their rarity, supernovas and novas have been seen and recorded for a very long time. It is reasonable to assume that astronomers in many regions of the ancient world, especially those of the Middle East, witnessed the appearance and disappearance of these stars. Unfortunately, their written accounts of these spectacular sky performers, if such were made, have proved elusive.

It remained for the ancient Chinese astronomers, however, to leave informative records of the occurrences of novas and supernovas. These records are still valuable to modern astronomers for purposes of checking. The earliest of the Chinese written accounts go back fourteen centuries before the Christian era. They were on oracle bones, one of the first writing materials used by ancient Chinese scholars. The bones are called "oracle" because they were used to predict the future. As their predictions became the past, they provided a record of events.

As a measure of the rarity of supernovas, the more interesting of the "guest stars," Chinese astronomers reported a colossal stellar bang in 1054. There was a second in 1572, seen and recorded by Tycho Brahe. Johannes Kepler, one of the Danish astronomer's assistants, reported a third in 1604. The supernova that caught and held the attention of Chinese astronomers at the Kaifeng Observatory had by far the most astronomical significance.

When first seen, the supernova was said to be a star of unusual brilliance, comparable to the brightness of the planet we now call Venus. For almost a month Chinese astronomers kept it under close watch, until it exploded with a spectacular display. The brilliance of the exploding star is believed to have been many times that of the sun. Through careful study of old Chinese astronomical records and their own precise calculations, modern astronomers have determined that the cosmic debris of this super bang may still be seen as the Crab Nebula in the constellation Taurus. The dust cloud of that once bright star is still a popular area for study by present-day astronomers using sophisticated radio telescopes.

There is probably no more beautiful astronomical sight than a flaming comet arching across the vault of a night sky. Flashing briefly into view on their endless space journeys, comets are also "guest stars." Well aware of the transistory nature of comets, Chinese astronomers preferred to call them "brush " or "broom " stars. No doubt they were inspired by the cloudlike tail of the space visitors.

Comets were quite familiar to astronomers of antiquity. The skilled sky observers of ancient Babylon left clay-tablet records about comets that date from 1140 B.C. However, Chinese astronomers of ancient times were the best observers and reporters of these phenomena. Their written accounts are the most extensive and accurate in existence.

After long and careful searching, scholars have found that, beginning as early as 613 B.C. and continuing into the early 1600s, Chinese astronomers saw and listed some 372 comets. They not only recorded the date of appearance of these guest stars, but also left descriptions of many of them. The astronomers would tell of such things as the length of time of a comet's visit, the brilliance and length of its tail, and, after some complex calculation, its path of flight. Incidentally, they were the first to notice and record that a comet's tail always pointed away from the sun.

Although astronomers of ancient China were quite meticulous about noting a number of characteristics of comets, they were far off the mark in explaining their origin. At various times in the annals of that country, astronomers indicated their belief that comets were parts of distant planets that had broken away and been flung into space.

Another idea, particularly popular during the earliest periods of Chinese astronomy, was the belief that comets were the result of Yin and Yang being out of balance. Throughout Chinese civilization Yin and Yang were considered fundamental forces of nature that influenced the cosmic world as well as every aspect of man's life on earth.

Best known of all the comets cited throughout the long history of astronomy is Halley's Comet. Edmund Halley was an English astronomer and mathematician of the mid-seventeenth century. One of his more outstanding achievements was the development and proof of the theory that comets return into our part of the universe periodically. He proved his idea with the discovery of a comet in 1682 that, Halley said, would come back in some seventy-odd years.

Before his death, Halley had said that the comet now bearing his name was the same one reported in 1531 and in 1607. The latter sighting had been made by Johannes Kepler. Halley's work excited astronomers everywhere. A number of them concentrated their own studies on this particular comet, mainly to find out how far back in time Halley's Comet had started its visits close to earth.

Since Chinese astronomical records were known to be the oldest and most extensive, researchers focused their attention on these. The astronomers' scholarly efforts produced some interesting findings. They discovered a vague reference to a comet that had flashed across the China sky in 467 B.C. Although strongly suspecting this was Halley's Comet, they were unable to find definite proof. Digging deeper into ancient Chinese astronomical records, researchers came upon still another account of a brilliant comet, this time from 240 B.C.

After studying the description given and carrying out some involved calculations, the researchers concluded that this was indeed Halley's Comet. Beginning in A.D. 66 and continuing to 1066, records on the visits of this celestial traveler were kept with remarkable regularity by Chinese astronomers.

A final word on comets. Halley's Comet is known to reappear about every seventy-six years. Its first blazing visit in our century took place in 1910. We can look forward to another spectacular peformance in 1986.

Solar and lunar eclipses make amateur astronomers out of most of us. During a full solar eclipse countless numbers will watch the sun disappearing and emerging from behind the moon. All sorts of emotions are aroused during a sighting, from fear to wonder about man's puny existence in the universe. Eclipses have been affecting people this way ever since we became aware of these astronomical phenomena.

In ancient times eclipses were fearful spectacles to most peoples and were generally believed to be signs of coming disasters. Among the Chinese the darkening of the sun or moon was believed to be the work of imaginary creatures inhabiting the cosmic world. One of their old myths tells of a three-legged crow who lives in the sun and from time to time eats the solar body, causing an eclipse. Another tale concerns a turtle inhabiting the moon who does the same thing, making it disappear at various times.

Other beliefs were common. Eclipses were considered the work of cosmic spirits that caused floods, famines, and devastating fires. Such catastrophes were the spirits' way of showing displeasure at actions of an emperor. And if a ruler was wise, he would soon mend his ways.

There is no doubt that Chinese astronomers gave a great deal of attention to eclipses at a very early date. Historians of ancient Chinese science have thus far been unable to determine precisely when these serious studies began. If the old legends and myths are taken into account, then Chinese scientists observed, recorded, and wondered about eclipses as far back as 3000 and 2000 B.C.

However, for more factual evidence, scholars prefer the messages they have interpreted from ancient oracle bones. These indicate that Chinese astronomers were recording lunar eclipses as early as 1361 B.C., 1342 B.C., and 1304 B.C. As for solar eclipses, they reported one taking place in 1217 B.C. The accounts are considered the oldest existing records of these astronomical events.

The Chinese astronomers were certainly not the only scientists to study eclipses. Those of ancient Chaldea (1000 B.C.–540 B.C.) and Greece were no less busy observing these phenomena. Indeed, Chaldean sky watchers made the important discovery that similar solar eclipses recur after intervals of 18 years and 11⅓ days. The saros cycle, as their finding became known, still serves astronomers for predicting eclipses.

Greek astronomers were also capable of making the same predictions about eclipses of the sun after learning of the saros cycle.

However, it remained for diligent Chinese astronomers to leave the richest legacy of knowledge concerning eclipses. Their careful records of these events are the oldest in existence. Of particular value to modern astronomers is a yearly listing of solar and lunar eclipses that Chinese sky observers started in 700 B.C. and continued to about the 1500s.

Chinese astronomers did not involve themselves in studies of eclipses solely for the purpose of obtaining pure knowledge. They sought information that could be applied to some practical use. This was a characteristic of their scientific activities that was directly opposite to the philosophy of Greek scientists. The latter pursued their studies of the unknown mainly for the satisfaction of knowledge alone. Observation and study of eclipses enabled Chinese astronomers to make an extremely accurate calendar that was vital to the interests of the people of that country.

Despite their interest in practical aims, Chinese astronomers were by no means indifferent to the scientific aspects of eclipses. Much of their time and effort was spent in explaining the nature of these celestial phenomena and in working out mathematically the mechanics of the repeated happenings. Among the earliest accounts of the reason for solar eclipses was that written by Liu Hsiang in 20 B.C. These events occurred, he said, when the moon moves across the sun and blots it out.

In the first century of the Christian era Chinese scholars were able to write that a lunar eclipse takes place when the sun's light upon the moon is blocked off by the earth passing between the two celestial bodies.

The astronomers' scientific explanation for eclipses had little effect on the common people. They still preferred to believe the myths and legends. Wang Ch'ung (circa 27–100) sought to discredit these by writing that eclipses were in no way associated with the cosmic spirits that brought on floods, famines, and other catastrophes. Nor was the emperor responsible for them. Solar and lunar eclipses, he contended, are regular occurrences that can be predicted.

Although unfamiliar with the saros cycle, Chinese astronomers developed their own method for predicting solar eclipses sometime in the first century B.C. By the seventh century A.D., after much refinement of their system, Chinese astronomers could predict solar eclipses with remarkable accuracy. They were able to foretell the exact day of these celestial events, the hour, and the times when the eclipse would begin and end.

Astronomy is one of the oldest scientific interests. And of all the ancient scholars who contributed to the preparation of the groundwork on which the present science is based, few did more than the skilled and methodical Chinese astronomers.

2. Ancient Chinese Medicine

Illness has always been a part of our existence on earth. Ancient peoples the world over practiced some form of healing the sick and injured. The work of administering treatments was confined to a small group of individuals who, for the most part, acquired their special knowledge and status from their parents. Others with a strong leaning toward the art of healing were selected and trained by the more experienced. They were the first doctors.

These ancient medical practitioners had very little in the way of effective medicines or techniques, so they did what was common among nearly all the peoples of the past: they sought the help of magic spirits. This ability to communicate with the spirit world made these early doctors enormously influential in their society. They were known by a variety of terms, like "shaman" or simply "medicine man" or "folk doctor."

As civilizations advanced and medical knowledge expanded, the role of magic in the healing arts became less and less important. It was never really abandoned, however, even though doctors were beginning to employ more practical methods. In the development and use of nonmagical healing techniques few societies in the ancient world excelled. The Greeks and Chinese may well have been the exceptions.

Separated by thousands of miles, the Chinese and Greek civilizations carried on their evolving medical activities quite independently of one another. Yet both made notable strides in the medical field at approximately the same period. This was the final half of the first millennium B.C.

It was Greek medicine that later formed the foundation for the development of this science in Europe. In all probability if China had not been so far distant, the practice of medicine there would also have been of interest to the West. This can be assumed from what has been taking place in Eastern and Western medicine in the past several decades. After more than two thousand years the West is beginning to appreciate the accomplishments of ancient Chinese medical practitioners. Some are proving of considerable value for today's art of healing. Others are being studied and tested.

Chinese doctors of antiquity never completely abandoned their practice of calling on the powers of the spirit world for help. However, the old simplistic beliefs had evolved into far more complex concepts involving cosmological forces. The doctrines of Yin and Yang and the five elements had become a basic part of Chinese medicine for both diagnosing and treating illness.

Yin and Yang represented the balance of energy in nature

Yin and Yang are considered cosmic energies that reside within the human body as well as throughout the universe. Yin is interpreted as negative — cold, dark, and female. Yang is positive — light, warm, and male. Though opposites, these forces are inseparable. Yin is in Yang; Yang is in Yin.

Yin and Yang are pictorially represented by a famous symbol known to most of us. It consists of a circle within which are two curved forms shaped like tadpoles. Fitting together exactly, they are in reverse positions. One form is generally pictured as white and the other black.

Since they are complements of one another, Yin and Yang never exist in an individual state. But one may be in excess of the other. It is this imbalance that causes ill health and unpleasant happenings in nature. While Yin and Yang remained in balance or harmony within an individual, good health prevailed. Once this balance was disturbed, causing illness, it was the Chinese physician's aim to restore harmony by whatever treatment he considered effective. The most common treatments in use in ancient China were acupuncture, herbal medicines, and moxabustion. Scholars believe that Chinese physicians were performing their duties on the basis of the Yin-Yang concept as early as the sixth century B.C.

The five-element theory was the second philosophical concept that strongly influenced the development of medicine in ancient China. Indeed, the doctrine pervaded nearly all early Chinese thought.

Very simply, the five-element theory maintained that everything was made of five elements — earth, wood, water, fire, and metal. An interrelationship existed between these elements as well as with human structure and function. When a person suffered illness there was a disharmony among the elements; good health meant all was in harmony. Guided by this belief, a physician treated the patient on the basis of whatever element or elements were in discord.

It is interesting that by the fifth century B.C. Greek philosophers had perfected a similar theory concerning the make-up of the physical world. Theirs was also a five-element system, but one that omitted wood. They identified the fifth as a kind of basic substance common to all elements.

In a somewhat more practical way the three great religions or philosophical systems generally associated with China — Confucianism, Taoism, and Buddhism — all left their mark on the art of healing in that land. Indeed, the philosophy and code of human behavior that the three systems expounded played a major role in the social and political affairs of the Chinese for more than two thousand years.

Confucianism had its beginning in the Chou Dynasty, which, from 1030 to 221 B.C., ruled a much smaller China than now exists. The philosophical system originated with K'ung Fu-Tzu, whom we know best by his Latinized name, Confucius. Born in 551 B.C. in the Province of Shantung, Confucius became one of ancient China's greatest scholars. His teachings brought him wide renown, and he was often called Master K'ung.

Confucius worked in government service for a time, even serving as an adviser to Emperor Chou. Growing disillusionment over the corrupt and pleasure-seeking ways of the royal court and the behavior of people in general caused Confucius to withdraw from society. He went into seclusion for several years to meditate on ethics and the attitudes of people.

By the time he ended his voluntary isolation, Confucius had formulated a philosophical system and a code of ethics. It applied to everyone, those in government as well as people in all walks of life. In time the system of human behavior Confucius created attracted many followers. His most eloquent disciples traveled far and wide through the land, exhorting people to mend their ways by heeding the word of Confucius. Their work as missionaries proved highly successful, and untold thousands became ardent supporters of the beliefs of this great scholar. Confucius died in 479 B.C., but his wisdom was to endure for more than two millennia.

One of the many precepts that Confucius urged people to observe was the forging of an everlasting bond of respect and remembrance between the living and the dead. From this rule of conduct came the belief that the human body, which had been received from one's parents, should not be mutilated. After death the body should be returned to one's ancestors in a complete, unmarred state.

Over the course of time this idea proved to be an obstacle to the development of surgery by Chinese physicians. Autopsies and dissections were forbidden, with the result that knowledge of human anatomy never reached the levels of other areas of ancient Chinese medicine.

As far as actual records tell us, there exist only two official accounts of dissections, in A.D. 16 and in 1106. Although we are not told anything about the subjects, in all likelihood they were executed criminals. It wasn't until comparatively modern times that Chinese physicians caught up with Western doctors in their knowledge of the human body.

Taoism was another great philosophical system that sprang up in early China. The followers of Taoism, disillusioned with the everyday world, believed that a fuller, more satisfying life could be attained only through the study and understanding of nature. Mixed with a little shamanism and some elementary science, Tao was "the Way" one should travel to achieve riches, long life, and happiness.

Lao Tzu was one of the founders of Taoism. We know little about his life except that he expounded brilliantly the precepts of what eventually became one of China's enduring religions. His teachings, set down sometime in the third century B.C., inspired countless of his countrymen to abandon their harsh, daily existence for the promise of a better life offered by Taoism.

Aside from purely philosophical exercises for attaining the better life, leaders of the Taoist movement, many of whom were scholarly monks, also busied themselves with scientific and technological interests. One of these areas of activity was alchemy, the forerunner of chemistry. They were drawn to this field of bubbling pots and potions by the hope of finding the elixir of life. This was believed to be a magic substance that would make life everlasting. Alchemists in the West pursued this will-o'-the-wisp with equal ardor.

Taoist scholars never did find the elixir, of course, but in pursuit of it they carried out experiments with a wide variety of herbs and, as a result, developed a number of preparations that proved helpful in treating illness. Many different kinds of minerals were also tested, including sulfur, arsenic, mercury, and zinc. Taoist alchemists successfully transformed these into healing ointments and salves.

Displaying a particularly keen interest in the medical field, Taoist scholars compiled a *Materia Medica* early in the third century A.D. In it were listed the medicines in use at the time, along with directions for making pills and powders. It was the first book of its kind that survived the long passage of time down to our own era.

Buddhism originated in India between the sixth and fifth centuries B.C. Its founder was Siddhartha Gautama, an ascetic scholar. As his teachings became widely accepted, a flourishing religion developed, and he was called the Buddha — the Enlightened One.

How or when Buddhism crossed the borders of ancient China we do not know. Many scholars believe it may have been at the time of Christianity's beginning. It is certain, however, that there was a small group of Buddhist monks established in northern Kiangsu in A.D. 65.

The teachings of Buddhism were a good deal more religious in tone than either Confucianism or Taoism. Very briefly, they maintained that life was a temporary state and suffering its chief characteristic. Desire was the driving force of existence and therefore the cause of suffering. Salvation, meaning the complete elimination of desire, can be achieved only through rigorous mental and physical practices. Not the least of these was meditation.

Buddhism won millions of followers, not only in China but throughout East Asia. After more than two thousand years of existence, it is still a vibrant religion, attracting adherents even in the West. During the early period of their existence in China, Buddhist monks had come with religious messages, or sutras, which eventually were translated into the Chinese language. But this wasn't all they brought. The work of Indian scientists, astronomers, mathematicians, and doctors was also introduced. Surgical techniques were foremost among their medical information. However, inhibited by the taboos of Confucianism concerning the human body, Chinese physicians did little with that knowledge.

It may be wondered how so much is known today of the nature of medical practice in ancient China. This fortunate development came about through the strong impulse of Chinese physicians to leave a record of their work. They wanted to tell others, especially those in future generations, of the kinds of illnesses existing in their time and the methods used for treating them. Of all the ancient peoples the Chinese are the only ones who left such a rich store of writings in the medical field.

The earliest of Chinese medical writings were discovered by archaeologists digging into China's past. The books unearthed were not like those we have today. They would not have lasted for more than twenty-five hundred years if they were. These ancient written accounts were oracle bones, the same kinds of records that provided information about supernovas and lunar eclipses.

Writings on these bones mention some of the more common ailments that afflicted people. The oracle bones also contained a number of the earliest known descriptions of plants with healing properties.

Of all the books that appeared during the early period of China's medical practice none acquired the popularity or endurance of the *I Ching*, or *Book of Changes*. It was an oracle book that exercised immense influence both on medicine and on other fields of human endeavor. The *Book of Changes* provided a complete system of divination concerning future events.

The system consisted of symbols made up of broken and unbroken lines. These could be formed with little sticks. The symbols were arranged into combinations of eight trigrams and sixty-four hexagrams, each called a *kua*. All were listed in a special order in the book. Farther along, the *Book* gave explanations for every *kua*.

An individual seeking advice, in medicine for example, would arrange the little sticks to form an appropriate symbol. Then he would turn to the explanation. This would be given in an abstract way, thus allowing the reader freedom to choose any interpretation desired.

The *Book of Changes* was not the work of a single writer. It was a collection of very ancient omens originating with Chinese farmers. Its origins may go back to the eighth century B.C. After many alterations, scholars believe the *Book* reached its final form in the third century B.C. Confucian scholars played a big role in putting the finishing touches to the work. This ancient collection became so popular that Chinese on all levels of society have continued to consult it for two thousand years.

In ancient China there were times when a doctor's position was little respected and even dangerous, regardless of his fame. This was the experience of Hua T'o, a noted physician who carried on his medical activities sometime in the second century B.C. Hua T'o had acquired his medical fame working among wounded soldiers on the battlefields. He was deeply disturbed by the pain the victims experienced, especially when efforts were made to help them. It was from this battlefield activity that the physician developed a primitive form of anesthesia, antedating a similar development in Western medicine by almost two thousand years.

We do not know the ingredients that Hua used for his anesthetic. The guess is that it must have been a mixture of herbs or other plant substances, since these were basic to the majority of ancient Chinese drugs. The herb or plant mixture was stirred vigorously with a liberal quantity of wine. A patient drinking the potion invariably fell into a sound sleep, oblivious of pain as the doctor worked on his wound.

Hua T'o had also become widely known for his general skill as a physician, not only as the creator of anesthesia. Emperor Ts'ao Ts'ao heard about him and one day sent a message, ordering the physician to come to the palace. It seemed the emperor suffered from chronic headaches, which the court physicians were unable to do anything about.

The folk doctor, for that was Hua's actual status, arrived at the palace. He examined the emperor, then prescribed some herbal medicines. In a very short time the emperor was free of his headaches. He was deeply impressed and requested the doctor to write a book describing everything he knew about illness and the treatments available. The emperor wanted this medical knowledge for his own private use. He also wanted Hua to join his staff of court physicians.

The doctor refused both the emperor's wishes. He had no desire to write about medicine; he preferred to carry on his medical work among the people, not for a small, select palace group. To refuse the emperor was no light matter. Ts'ao became furious and promptly ordered the doctor thrown into jail. When a period of confinement failed to change Hua's mind, the executioners were ordered to sharpen their axes.

While in jail Hua had become bored with nothing to do and decided to write the medical book the emperor had wanted. But it would not be for the emperor. Hua had other plans.

He began to put into writing everything he knew about ailments and the best methods for treating them. He also gave a detailed description of the formula for the anesthetic he had created.

When Hua T'o finished his manuscript he tried to make an arrangement with his jailer to have it taken to a member of his family. Folk medicine in ancient China was a family affair, handed down from father to son. But the jailer refused. At that, Hua became enraged and tore the manuscript into pieces. Thus ended what might have been a valuable contribution to the medical field, certainly from the historical standpoint. Equally unfortunate was the permanent loss of the formula for what was probably the first effective form of anesthesia.

Scholars have found in their studies of ancient Chinese medicine that the most important books on the subject were written during the second and first centuries B.C. Most of these classic writings had also begun to differ from those written in earlier ages. The books were now more encyclopedic in scope, ranging over the whole field of medicine and including metaphysical and natural forces related to illness, the different kinds of illnesses, and the variety of treatments.

Of all the medical books to appear in the period mentioned above or, in fact, in any other period of China's history, none equaled in greatness the *Huang Ti Nei Ching*. This has undergone a number of translations, one of the more popular being *The Yellow Emperor's Classic on Internal Medicine*. Its origin is obscure. Some believe it was the work of Huang Ti, the Yellow Emperor, a legendary ruler who reigned in the second millennium B.C. Scholars, however, prefer to pinpoint *Nei Ching*'s origin as some time between 479 and 300

B.C. A number of writers undoubtedly had a hand in compiling the book's information, making changes and additions. The last of these were made between A.D. 1068 and 1078.

The *Nei Ching* has been compared to a similar compilation of medical treatises in the West, the Hippocratic collection. This too was a storehouse of medical knowledge, put together by the famous Greek physician Hippocrates; it appeared at approximately the same time as the *Nei Ching,* between 450 and 350 B.C. The Hippocratic collection remained the foundation of Western medical practice for many centuries. The *Nei Ching* became the "bible" for Chinese medicine over a span of more than two thousand years. This Chinese medical classic acquired international fame when it appeared in a French version in 1957.

Many aspects of medical knowledge were covered in the *Nei Ching.* For example, it sought to explain in metaphysical terms the connection between the forces of nature and the ills mankind experiences; it suggested ways for maintaining good health, as through proper breathing exercises; and it presented the first detailed description of acupuncture.

Like a number of ancient Chinese medical procedures, practically nothing is known about the beginning of acupuncture. That it is very old there is no doubt. The unique treatment may already have existed during China's Stone Age. Evidence of this has been the discovery of flint needles used in the treatment. Acupuncture may also have been used first by the sha-

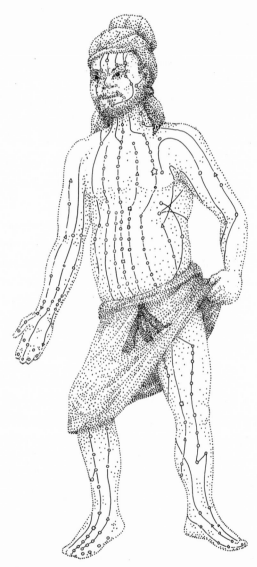

An acupuncture chart

mans, the witch doctors who controlled Chinese medical practice in the Stone Age, to drive demons from the body of a sick person. During later periods of China's history, in the Iron and Bronze Ages, flint needles gave way to those of metal.

Very simply, acupuncture is a form of therapy in which one needle or several needles are inserted into a patient's skin. The needles may penetrate the skin to varying depths and at particular points of the body. The points are usually arranged in what are called meridian lines.

In employing acupuncture for treating chronic backaches or headaches, for example, doctors of ancient China believed they were restoring Yin and Yang to a balanced state within the patient. The needles accomplished this by letting out of the body an excess of Yin or Yang, or putting back into the body whichever force was lacking. For most illnesses, acupuncture consisted of a series of treatments.

Acupuncture must have proved effective over the passage of time, enduring as it has for more than three thousand years. In recent times the treatment has gone beyond China's borders and is being used in many countries of the world.

For today's acupuncture treatment doctors use three kinds of needles, most of which are made of a steel alloy. One has an extremely thin insertion point, another has a triple-sided cutting edge, and finally there is a so-called skin needle. This has a cluster of six points at the insertion end and is used mostly for treating children. The needle is not inserted; it is simply tapped over the child's skin. Tests are also being performed with a newly developed electric acupuncture needle.

The doctor administering acupuncture must know exactly the various points on the patient's body where the needles should be inserted. He must be equally aware of the correct position in which to place the patient's body; the proper angle and technique for inserting the needles, and the effective duration of the treatment.

Acupuncture needles may be inserted in a variety of ways, depending on the kind of stimulation the doctor wishes to arouse in a patient. A needle may be twirled or jabbed quickly into the skin, or it may be inserted slowly, in rhythm with a patient's breathing. Whatever the technique, there is no pain.

A secondary form of acupuncture, which grew out of the original, is called natural acupuncture. Instead of needles, finger pressure is applied along the meridian lines of a patient's body. It is sometimes used for minor headaches or toothache.

Western doctors first became aware of Chinese acupuncture treatment in the late seventeenth century, when a Dutch physician published a medical paper on the subject. Fellow doctors were little impressed, however, and acupuncture became nothing more than an item of passing interest.

In the nineteenth century, the Western medical profession changed its feelings somewhat regarding acupuncture. The physician father of Hector Berlioz, a noted French composer, was largely responsible for this development. After using it on a number of his patients with good results, he wrote an enthusiastic paper on acupuncture for the benefit of his medical colleagues. This time they were not so quick to dismiss it, since they noticed the positive results on their patients.

In the 1950s acupuncture began to receive serious attention by physicians in the United States. Since that time many have received training on the theory and techniques of acupuncture. A sizable group feels that this ancient Chinese medical technique is a definite contribution to the healing art of today. Others are not convinced, because when they made use of acupuncture the results were far from what they had been led to expect.

However, there is a greater consensus on the value of acupuncture in certain special applications, as an anesthetic, for example. In modern China acupuncture is frequently employed for this purpose, even in cases of major surgery. Western doctors who have used or witnessed the use of acupuncture as an anesthetic believe it has some advantage over the Western practice of administering painkilling drugs. Sometimes drugs can produce an unfavorable side effect on a patient.

Moxabustion, or moxa, as it is also known, is an equally old Chinese medical treatment. Like acupuncture, moxa was a kind of stimulation therapy, but it used fire instead of needles. A doctor would pulverize the dried leaves of the mugwort plant (*Artemisia vulgaris*) and roll the substance into the shape of a small cone. Several cones would be placed at specific spots on the patient's body, almost the same areas as those used for acupuncture needles, and then ignited.

The burning cones were removed just before the fire touched the patient's skin; that is, if the doctor was paying attention to his job. Otherwise, the unhappy victim would soon let the physician know with a loud "Ouch!" that the treatment wasn't going well. The idea behind moxabustion was to cause an intense stimulation of the blood and nerves in the areas treated. A red spot beneath the burning cone was the physical evidence of this stimulation.

Western medical practice today employs basically the same idea with the application of heat for certain muscular aches. The modern heat-producing devices, however, like the electric pad, are a far cry from the burning cones.

Over the years powdered mugwort leaves gave way to other plant substances for making moxabustion cones. These included mulberry leaves, also used for silk production, ginger, and aconite (monkshood). Although modern medical practice has largely replaced folk medicine in China, many of the old treatments still survive, particularly in the remote rural areas. Moxabustion is one of these. But like many of the old practices, it too has changed.

When treating a patient today, doctors more often than not are apt to place a piece of garlic or onion under the cone of powdered leaves. These additions beneath the cone protect a patient from burning and also have some healing value. Garlic especially is believed to be effective in helping to relieve pain and in curing some pulmonary ailments, like asthma and bronchitis. Garlic for medicinal use is not unique to Chinese physicians; the pungent seasoner is almost universally used for that purpose.

Because doctors in ancient China had little knowledge of human anatomy or of functions of the body, their approach toward diagnosing illnesses, especially internal kinds, seems to us bewildering. Deductions were largely based on cosmological factors as well as various external signs that appeared on a patient's body.

Internal ailments were the most difficult for the Chinese physician to diagnose, yet he was never at a loss when it came to telling a patient the nature of a problem. It seems that over the course of many years Chinese medical practitioners had standardized numerous unusual external signs on the human body that in some mysterious fashion were related to certain internal organs. Thus, if a doctor noted that a patient's eyes were dark gray in color, he diagnosed the illness as a disease of the kidneys. Signs on ears and tongue were related to disorders of the spleen, lungs, and heart.

But these signs of illness were only secondary tools that helped a Chinese physician diagnose a patient's ailment. His most important aid was the taking of the pulse. No one knows when Chinese doctors began using the pulse to tell them about the inner workings of the human body. However, it was being written about as early as 500 B.C.

The pulse was mentioned as a diagnostic tool by the noted physician Pien Ch'io in his *Nan Ching*, a classic medical work. He assigned various characteristics to the pulse, which was supposed to reveal something about internal illnesses. "The pulse is like scattered leaves of trees, like fire-grass — like a taut thread." That most famous of all ancient Chinese medical classics, the *Nei Ching*, contains descriptions of the pulse as "drum" pulse and "breathless" pulse.

The Chinese physician located the pulse at a number of places on the human body. It was most commonly taken, however, at the head, foot, and, of course, the wrists. The wrist pulse gave the Chinese doctor a great deal of information. The pulse was taken in three different places on each wrist. Feeling the pulse at one point on the right wrist helped the physician determine if the patient was suffering from a lung ailment. A certain spot on the left wrist gave signs on the condition of a patient's heart. A second location on the right wrist was supposed to reveal some problem with a patient's heart. And so it went.

The whole diagnostic procedure employed by Chinese physicians in ancient times was exceedingly complicated and far from accurate. Nevertheless, their methods for determining the nature of an illness, particularly by checking the pulse, had some value. In the modern world of medicine the pulse is a valuable indicator of a patient's condition.

Although there is no solid evidence supporting the idea, it is interesting to speculate that by "reading" the pulse ancient Chinese medical practitioners may have discovered circulation within the human body. If so, this would have been more than two thousand years before Western physicians knew about the blood flowing through the arteries and veins. It was not until early in the seventeenth century that the English physician William Harvey first explained the circulation of the blood.

What might be called the medical phase of diagnosis as performed by doctors in ancient China was only part of the long-drawn-out procedure. Before any treatment began for a determined illness, the cosmological phase of diagnosis had to be taken into account. Were the stars in the correct position for the patient? Was the patient in harmony with the season of the year? The day? The hour? Only when these and other factors were considered to the physician's satisfaction did treatment begin.

Acupuncture and moxabustion were two of the more common treatments. Massage was another. But the most frequently used of all was the prescribing of medicines, or drugs. Herbs and other plant substances were the chief ingredients of Chinese medicines. Some were made of animal and mineral elements. Indeed, it would not be too far wrong to say that just about everything in the world of the Chinese, plant and animal, was a candidate for conversion into a medicine for human needs.

Literally thousands of substances were used by the

pharmacists of ancient China to formulate medicines. In the sixteenth century a book on drugs recorded more than two thousand basic substances that were being employed for over sixteen thousand medicines. A vast number of these were sheer oddities that did little, if anything, to give a person relief from an ailment. A few of these included powdered teeth and bones of fossilized mammoths, known as "dragon teeth," the contents of the stomachs of musk oxen, and scorpions.

The doctors of ancient China could not explain in scientific terms why many of their herbal medicines were effective. Their keen sense of observation and, of course, the positive reactions of patients were all that enabled them to tell how or why the herbal drugs worked. If further explanation was needed, they would refer to the indivisible relationship between the life forces of nature and man.

Drugs were prescribed in harmony with the Chinese theory of the five elements. Everything in nature was made of the same five elements — fire, wood, water, metal, and earth. Medicines made of ingredients specifically related to one of these elements were given for ailments originating in those parts of the human body which were similarly related. For example, if the source of an illness was centered in the heart or kidneys, which Chinese physicians believed were associated with fire and water respectively, then only medicines related to those elements were prescribed.

All parts of medicinally valuable herbs and other plants were used in the making of a drug — blossoms, leaves, seeds, roots, and fruit. Various processes were employed for preserving these ingredients, including drying, roasting, and soaking in water. They were also used in a fresh state. Just a sampling of the vast number of plants used by the Chinese pharmacist included camphor, lobelia, mint, dandelion, and ginseng.

Ginseng was by far the most commonly used medicinal plant in ancient China. Even in present-day China, it is much sought after. The reason for this was the belief that the root of the plant had magical qualities for prolonging life. In ancient times it was popularly referred to as the "herb of eternal life."

The peculiar appearance of the ginseng plant had a great deal to do with the Chinese belief that it had magical powers. The root has a form that resembles the human figure. The bottom portion separates into two extensions that look like "legs." The upper part has two extensions resembling "arms."

The ginseng continues to be popular today, but for its true medicinal properties, not magic. Modern research on the plant has shown it to have a beneficial effect on the human body's central nervous system; it can help reduce high blood pressure, aid circulation, and provide a measure of relief to sufferers of diabetes.

While the ginseng plant was prized for its magical powers, the ephedra plant was held in greater esteem for its real medical worth by doctors of ancient China. The plant yielded a fluid, *mahuang*, that pharmacists

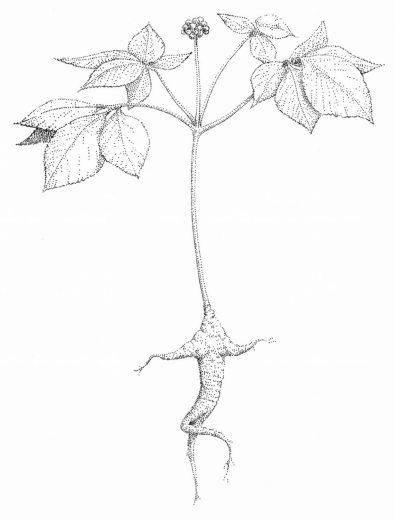

Ginseng

made into a potent drug. Doctors found this to be highly effective for reducing excessive bleeding and relieving coughing caused by asthma. The drug was in use as far back as two thousand years before the Christian era.

It is interesting that Greek physicians of ancient times were also familiar with the medicinal value of ephedra. Since they were hardly aware of China's existence, the likelihood is that they discovered the drug from the plant independently. European and American doctors did not become aware of ephedrine, as the drug is now known, until the early 1920s.

The store of modern drugs is enormous. Yet ephedrine, with a heritage of more than three millennia, remains unsurpassed for its ability to constrict blood vessels and stop excess bleeding. And it continues to be highly effective for freeing the clogged passages of asthma sufferers.

In 1924, Carl Frederic Schmidt, an American physician, was doing research at the Peking Union Medical College. He was investigating herbal substances that had been used for centuries in Chinese medicines. The youthful doctor's aim was to find some that had practical medical value and could be incorporated into the pharmacopoeia of Western medicine. After testing hundreds, he finally settled on a half-dozen that had promise. Of these, ephedra proved to be the best.

The second most important group of substances for medicines in ancient China was animal in origin. Just about every creature known to the Chinese, ranging from the rhinoceros to the toad, was a likely candidate for some kind of drug ingredient.

Many of these, as with some of the plant substances, were totally lacking in medical value. Others were effective, but the scientific explanations for their being so had to wait for modern laboratory testing techniques. A secretion from the skin of toads was an example. Chinese doctors used the substance for stimulation purposes. When subjected to modern laboratory analysis, the secretion was found to have the characteristics of adrenalin. Modern doctors prescribe adrenalin in a medically prepared form as a heart stimulant.

Another drug of animal origin, highly popular was "dragon teeth," made from the ground bones and teeth of prehistoric animals. The drug, though useless as medicine, made a helpful contribution to another and quite remote field of science, archaeology. When archaeologists spotted the prehistoric teeth and bones on the pharmacists' shelves and were told they had been unearthed by farmers tilling the soil, they lost little time launching digs at the sites. A number of valuable discoveries about the past were made in this manner.

Minerals were more the playthings of alchemists than of pharmacists. Nevertheless, a number of these substances were used to make effective drugs. Mercury was one of the common ones. When incorporated in an ointment, it was effectively used for ulcerated sores. Sulfur was another that, as part of a salve, helped to heal skin disorders. Arsenic was the base of an ointment used for skin rashes and sores. For bladder disorders, zinc sulfate was commonly prescribed. After centuries of use these and other minerals still play an important role in the modern pharmacists' armamentarium.

Other minerals less frequently used by pharmacists of ancient China were alum, gold, silver, and even such gems as rubies and amethysts.

Chinese physicians of ancient times did not limit their practice solely to the treatment of ailments. They were equally concerned with preventive medicine. How to keep people healthy and free of contagious diseases absorbed a great deal of their study and effort. In this connection, they were centuries ahead of their medical colleagues in the West. It has been only since the midpoint of this century that Western medical experts have begun to shift more of the emphasis of their work from healing to prevention, focusing largely on nutrition.

Nutrition — eating proper foods carefully prepared — exercise, and mental serenity were major aspects of a program that Chinese physicians advocated for a healthful life.

As for keeping people free of disease, Chinese doctors of ancient times had one outstanding achievement to their credit. They had developed a primitive form of vaccination to protect people from smallpox, a devastating disease in antiquity and up to recent times.

The variolation method they had worked out involved the removal of a small amount of the contents from the pustule of a smallpox victim. The material, transformed into a powder, was sniffed up the nose by a person seeking immunity from the disease.

By the eighteenth century Western medicine finally caught up with this fundamental idea for immunizing against contagious diseases. Edward Jenner, an English physician, discovered that by inoculating people with cowpox, he could prevent the dreaded smallpox from spreading.

Chinese doctors who acquired a great deal of knowledge and skill in preventive medicine were considered the greatest in their profession, which consisted of two main groups — folk doctors and doctors attached to the emperor's court. Folk doctors were traditionalists. They came from families where the knowledge and skill of medical practice had been handed down over many generations. Much of what they knew, especially the preparation of certain drugs, was a closely guarded secret. Folk doctors carried on their work almost exclusively among the peasants.

Physicians at the royal court were a different group entirely. A young man who aspired to a medical career at court received his training at schools established specifically for that purpose. One of the earliest of these was functioning in 84 B.C. By the third and fourth centuries there were a number of these medical training centers. The first medical school in Europe did not appear until the ninth century, at Salerno, Italy.

In ancient China the court physician's job was considered no different from any other government position. Thus, a candidate had to pass a written examination to show that he was qualified. Indeed, China was the first country to institute such a procedure for those seeking government jobs. The requirement was already in existence as far back as 165 B.C. Europe did not adopt the idea until A.D. 1140, when Roger II, Norman king of Sicily, introduced the practice.

The development of medical practice in ancient China was almost entirely a domestic affair. Few contributions to its advancement came from beyond the borders of that ancient land. It was during the First Opium War with Great Britain, 1839-1842, that Chinese doctors had their first encounter with medical practices of the West. What they saw did not exactly overwhelm them. They continued to believe that many of their methods and medicines were certainly as good as, and perhaps even superior to, those of Western practice.

However, in the late 1860s, as the contacts of Chinese doctors with the West expanded, their attitude changed. They were impressed by a number of features of Western medicine — the use of anesthesia, for example, and surgical techniques. As we know, surgery was the one area in Chinese medical practice that had been almost totally neglected.

In the twentieth century, the practitioners of traditional Chinese medicine received a real shock. The old dynastic rule had ended with the Manchu emperors, and by the mid-1920s a republican form of government, led by the Kuomintang Party, was attempting to run the country.

The new leaders of China were greatly disturbed by the backwardness of their country in science, technology, and medicine. To encourage the adoption of Western medical procedures, government leaders issued a ban on the traditional ways of healing. Chinese doctors were required to learn and use Western medical techniques. The ban was a failure. People, particularly those in remote rural areas, were reluctant to accept the new treatments or medicines. These were looked upon with suspicion. The people were comfortable with the old ways of treating ailments and had no desire to give them up.

Following World War II and the rise to power of the Communist Party under Mao Tse-tung, traditional Chinese medical practices were revived. Today there is an admixture of Chinese and Western traditional medicine. The best of two worlds had been integrated.

The adoption of medical techniques has not been a one-way flow into China. The West has also received some help from Chinese traditional methods, acupuncture being a case in point. Western medical researchers are also investigating the hundreds of herbs and other plant and animal substances used for centuries to make Chinese medicines. It is their hope that many of these substances will play important roles in the pharmacopoeia of the West, perhaps even in the seemingly futile fight against cancer.

3. Physical and Biological Sciences

Magnetism

Aside from the fact that some materials had the ability to attract metal objects, peoples of ancient times knew little about magnetism. The phenomenon was first discovered during some dim period in the prehistoric past in a rock called lodestone. This is scientifically known as magnetite, a form of iron ore naturally endowed with magnetic characteristics. Lodestone occurs in many places throughout the world but is believed by historians to have been found first by the inhabitants of Magnesia, an ancient name for a region that is now part of western Turkey.

Historical accounts tell us that the first attempt to explain the natural phenomenon in a scientific manner was made by Thales of Miletus some time in the sixth century B.C. Thales, a Greek philosopher who was also a skilled mathematician and astronomer, did not have much more to say about magnetism beyond the obvious fact that it was a power that attracted certain metal objects. In the view of some historians this may have been due to the general attitude of Greek philosophers toward particular subjects of science, such as magnetism. They considered this one of nature's insignificant occurrences, not worthy of extensive study. The Greek scholars preferred to concentrate on grander matters, like astronomy and mathematics. It remained for the scholars of ancient China to present the first record of the physical aspects of magnetism.

Like other areas of the world, China had its deposits of lodestone. When this mineral's odd behavior became known to the scholars of that land, their curiosity about it was aroused. For over eight centuries, Chinese scholars accumulated some interesting facts about magnetism. The time span of their activities covered the late Han and Sung Dynasties, when some of the most brilliant intellectual and technological achievements took place.

One of their more important discoveries was that a magnet had two poles; that is, if it was allowed to rotate freely, it would line up along a north-south line. The north or south poles of two magnets would push each other away, but the north pole of one magnet would be drawn to the south pole of the other. In other words, like poles repel; opposite poles attract. Western scientists did not become aware of polarity until about A.D. 500.

Scholars of ancient China also found the inductive ability of lodestone. They were able to make a non-magnetic piece of iron magnetic simply by rubbing it with lodestone. Similarly, they discovered long before scientists in the West that an iron object, such as a needle, could be magnetized if it were subjected to very high heat, lined up in a north-south direction and then, while held in this position, plunged into cold water to cause a quick drop in temperature. This is a process modern physicists call thermoremanence.

What Chinese scholars had learned about magnetism was pretty much the extent of knowledge on the subject until the sixteenth and seventeenth centuries, when European scientists became seriously interested in the phenomenon. Johannes Kepler (1571–1630), the noted German astronomer who worked with Tycho Brahe, compared gravity to magnetism. Bodies fall to the ground because the earth is like an enormous magnet pulling them downward.

William Gilbert (1544–1603), an English medical doctor and physicist, associated magnetism with the movement of the planets and stars. These were drawn on their directional paths by magnetic force. Even the great English physicist Isaac Newton (1642–1727) reached his revolutionary conclusions about gravity after first noting the strong parallelism between gravity and magnetism.

But the real scientific basis of magnetism was established in the nineteenth century, when such distinguished European scientists as James Clerk Maxwell (1831–1879), probing deep into the subject, proposed electromagnetic theories.

The polarity of magnetism was unquestionably the

greatest of the facts unearthed by Chinese scholars. Ultimately, the knowledge led Chinese technologists to create one of the most significant inventions, the compass. How this truly invaluable device was achieved will concern us later when Chinese technical triumphs are discussed.

Mathematics

Scholars of ancient China were deeply interested in mathematics, no less than those of Greece and India. Both of these countries were important centers in the ancient world for the early development of various forms of mathematics. And like Greek and Indian scholars, Chinese mathematicians made substantial contributions to the advancement of this purest of all the sciences.

Being extremely practical-minded, Chinese mathematicians were interested in numerical calculations almost solely for their usefulness. How best could the science of numbers help in the performance of such government activities as collecting taxes, or in the day-to-day affairs of the people, as in the marketplace. These were some of the things that made Chinese scholars want to improve the system of numbers.

Along with astronomy, mathematics played a major role in ancient China in the preparation of the calendar. Mathematicians worked side by side with astronomers at this task. Together they had worked out the division of the year into 365.25 days. This same figure, incidentally, when changed to degrees (365.25°), was used by Chinese mathematicians for dividing the circle, not the 360° of today.

There were many other areas in China's ancient civilization where the knowledge of mathematicians was applied. They would frequently be called on to make land surveys for the construction of roads and bridges, provide measurements in the building of a granary, and, just as today, help the government work out a system for taxing the people.

Two of the principal forms of mathematics applied to practical tasks in ancient China were simple numerical calculations and algebra. The numerical or digital system was most common. It began with the Chinese, as with people elsewhere in the world, when they learned to use their fingers for counting. No one can really say exactly when this bit of intelligence first entered the human mind.

During the second or first centuries B.C., the period of the early Han Dynasty, the Chinese were using a system for transforming finger numerical values into a written form. They indicated written number values by various combinations of short, straight lines. For example, the number 753 would be written as ⊥ ||||| ||| . This place value system had no zero, which had yet to come into existence. For a figure where a zero ordinarily would be needed, such as 50 or 100, the Chinese simply left one or more spaces.

The zero, so essential to modern mathematics, was created by the scholars of India. Its use in that country has been traced back as far as the ninth century A.D. Chinese mathematicians did not become familiar with the zero until the middle of the thirteenth century A.D. Ch'in Chiu-Shao, a celebrated mathematician of that era, was among the earliest to employ it.

Every student of mathematics learns quickly about *pi* — that it represents the ratio of the circumference of a circle to its diameter. The current value for *pi* is 3.14159265, a figure not very different from the one arrived at by Chinese mathematicians as early as the third century A.D. Liu Hui, one of many mathematicians concerned with this problem, had come very close to the current figure.

Chinese scholars also explored the more complex areas of mathematics. In so doing they later surprised their counterparts in the West by having covered ground that the latter felt was being studied for the first time. An example is the well-known Pascal triangle. This is made up of certain numbers placed in a triangular pattern. Each number within the triangle is equal to the sum of the two numbers above it, to the right and left. The arrangement serves as a mathematical key for determining the probable number of times a particular mathematical factor, or combination of such factors, may occur. For example, the probability of rolling a seven in dice within a limited series of throws can be worked out with the use of the Pascal triangle. The mathematical creation was the work of a brilliant French mathematician and philosopher, Blaise Pascal (1623–1662).

Gamblers were the first to use the Pascal triangle, in an effort to enhance their winnings. A more serious application was its role in the development of the modern theory of probability, which Pascal also helped to formulate. This has become a vital tool for statistical work in such fields as medical research, engineering, and insurance, where it is employed for formulating probability tables, like the life span of particular groups.

By the seventeenth century European scholars were gradually becoming aware of the intellectual accomplishments of the Chinese. This was due in large measure to the writings of Marco Polo about his travels in China and the reports of Jesuit missionaries residing in that land. It was in the course of this development that European mathematicians were astonished to learn that the Pascal triangle representation of binomial coefficients had already been worked out by Chinese students of mathematics in 1100 A.D., a good five centuries before the French scholar.

European students of higher mathematics were no less surprised to learn that the Chinese had developed algebra to an extremely advanced stage. Indeed, today's historians hold that Chinese mathematicians were using a form of algebra unequaled in the ancient world.

Mechanical Counters

Fingers were the first counting aids, used universally by the ancient peoples. What could be more readily available or simple for calculating in the marketplace, figuring tax payments or the number of days before the start of a festival? The use of fingers, in some instances even toes, for arithmetical calculations was a perfectly natural development.

Finger-counting among the ancient Chinese was far from a simple system, as one might assume. They used three variations. The first, and least complicated, was merely an extension of the full fingers. The second system, more complex, involved the joints of the fingers, to which numbers were assigned. In the third, and the most intricate of all, numbers were indicated by different positions of the fingers, the counter bending them or extending them in various combinations.

The first finger-counting method was the most widely used, particularly in the marketplace. In some areas of the world this method is still practiced today. In China the simple finger-counting method also developed into a highly popular children's game called *nuo ch'uan.* Two players extend their fingers simultaneously while at the same time guessing how many are extended. The player calling the correct number is the winner.

This finger game is not exclusively Chinese. It is played the world over with variations. American children and adults use an odd-or-even version of the finger game to determine, for example, which team is to bat first in a softball game. Two players, one from each of the opposing teams, extend one or two fingers while calling out "Odd" or "Even." The player who guesses correctly leads his team to bat first.

The second method of finger-counting, involving the joints, was used throughout ancient China and other parts of East Asia for all sorts of calculating purposes. These ranged from trading in the marketplace to the work of mathematicians and astronomers making a new calendar or revising an old one for the emperor.

The third and most complex counting method, involving various positions of the fingers and their combinations, is believed to have come to China from the Middle East. The Chinese refined the technique to the point where they were using it for decimal calculations.

Finger-counting methods in ancient China were supplemented and eventually almost totally displaced by devices that were truly mechanical. One of the earliest of these was the knotted string. This counting aid was described in written accounts as far back as the third century B.C. The use of knotted strings for counting was not unique to the Chinese. It came into existence independently among other peoples throughout the world. Perhaps the best-known users of the knotted string were the natives of Peru, who called it *quipu*. It is still employed in remote parts of that country.

Counting rods were another mechanical aid used by the Chinese for calculating. These were slim rods, about six inches long, made of bamboo, bone, ivory, or iron. Iron counting rods came into existence in the ninth century. Counting rods were either plain or marked with numbers. The marked rods were in wide use in the fourth century B.C. They were used for more than simple numerical problems; counting rods permitted the user to calculate volumes, weights, and

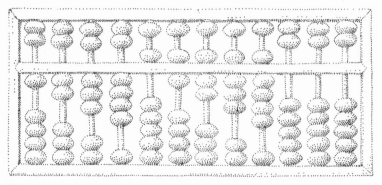

Abacus

lengths. Because they enabled the counter to work to remarkably close length measurements, counting rods were especially popular with engineers building roads, canals, and bridges. By the seventeenth century, during the Ming Dynasty, counting rods had almost passed out of existence. They had been replaced by another counting aid that proved far superior, the abacus.

No one really knows where the abacus originated. There is confusing evidence that points to several possible countries, with India the most likely candidate. In any case, the instrument did not reach China earlier than the middle of the fifteenth century. The abacus became popular throughout China because it lent speed and accuracy to those solving simple arithmetical problems as well as those of a more complicated nature.

Shortly after the end of World War II, while American forces were occupying Japan, a test between an abacus and an electric calculating machine was conducted in Tokyo. The abacus was used by an experienced clerk and the calculator by an American soldier. The clerk won handily in speed and accuracy, except in multiplication problems. The abacus is still popular in China and other countries of the Far East, the Middle East, and Russia.

Geography

Chinese in the pre-Christian era and for centuries after were not great travelers. They had little interest in going beyond the bounds of their land to see what other parts of the world were like. In this respect they were quite different from the Westerners, who roamed the far corners of the earth, seeking lands to conquer, riches, and knowledge.

Part of the reason for the Chinese attitude was their philosophical concept of the world. They considered their vast land the center of the universe. All the things for their daily living activities were readily at hand. And where else could the natural beauty of their land be surpassed?

There were other more down-to-earth reasons why the Chinese of ancient times were reluctant to travel beyond the frontiers of their country. Vast deserts, rugged mountains, and other natural hazards made journeying to distant places enormously difficult. As though these obstacles were not enough, there were always bandits ready to pounce on unwary travelers.

All this is not to say that the Chinese were totally without interest in far-off places. They did undertake caravan treks to far lands that often took months to complete. Nor did they refuse to welcome visitors from foreign countries. The latter came in friendship to exchange cultural, political, commercial, and even scholarly information. It was against this background, however, that Chinese scholars did so poorly in advancing geographical knowledge.

A change occurred about the time of the early Han Dynasty (202 B.C.–A.D. 9), when one of the Han emperors sent an official mission to lands far to the southwest of China. Members of the group were to explore and report on new regions and to offer friendship to the inhabitants of these areas. Written accounts of what this mission accomplished have long since disappeared. Nevertheless, it is believed that the party of explorers reached as far as the shore of the Indian Ocean.

This early Chinese expedition was followed by others. In A.D. 250, for example, the prince governing the Province of Wu dispatched a large mission headed by two ambassadors, again in the direction of the Indian Ocean. Small portions of the records kept by this mission have survived, indicating that the members of the group covered an immense amount of territory.

They visited Ceylon, India, and, some scholars believe, even traveled as far as the western part of the Arabian Peninsula. Among the wondrous things seen and learned about, aside from mountains, rivers, and forested regions, were merchant ships sailing regularly

between ports of different countries. This was novel to
the Chinese, since in their land most water traffic was
confined to rivers and canals. It was only during the
thirteenth, fourteenth, and fifteenth centuries that
China's maritime activity, coastwise and to foreign
lands, grew to dramatic proportions. This Chinese
mission was also much interested in noting the regularity of the monsoon season and the widespread existence of yet another religion, Hinduism.

Others who brought geographical knowledge back
to China were pilgrims who journeyed to India to wor-
ship at Buddhist shrines. The second and third centuries witnessed a particularly heavy stream of such
travelers.

In the course of such explorations as the above, Chinese geographers of ancient times slowly acquired a
store of information about lands extending to the
Middle East and what we know today as Manchukuo,
Korea, and Japan. Visitors to China helped to expand
this knowledge. Merchants and envoys of good will
from southern countries like Burma, Cambodia, and
Thailand came to pay their respects to Chinese emperors. Long before Marco Polo's historic journey to
China in the 1300s, visitors from the eastern part of the
Roman Empire in the second century A.D. brought
messages of friendship to the rulers of the Han Dynasty.

These geographical activities were only part of the
overall studies by Chinese scholars. Indeed, by far the
greater portion of their interest in geography had to do

with their own country. They compiled detailed, written accounts of the terrain, often accompanied by maps. In ancient China maps were surprisingly common and were drawn for a number of different uses. The ruling emperors often called on geographic scholars and mapmakers to give them maps showing the borders of their domain. Government officials in charge of the various provinces needed maps detailing the farming areas, villages, rivers, and other land features. Maps were extremely important for military commanders preparing campaigns of conquest or defense against hostile invaders. One such military map, drawn in 99 B.C. by a conquering general and forwarded to his emperor, showed the route he and his army had marched, across rivers, mountains, and other rugged obstacles. Finally, and of a more peaceful character, maps in ancient China were drawn to show caravan routes and the distances between rest stations.

The greatest of China's early mapmakers was P'ei Hsiu (A.D. 234–271), head of the Ministry of Public Works. Maps were essential for his work, but unfortunately, those available to him were completely unsatisfactory. They were poorly drawn, often neglecting to show mountains, farming areas, and villages properly. More important, the maps were drawn in such a manner that it was impossible to locate accurately the main features of the regions they covered. There was only one solution to the problem. P'ei decided to draw his own maps.

P'ei's map-drawing project was no simple undertaking. It was an atlas, actually, consisting of eighteen maps. Each map depicted a portion of China as the country existed in the third century. The countries bordering China, which the Chinese considered barbaric, were also represented.

P'ei drew his maps on the basis of the ancient Chinese cosmological belief that the earth was square. But the maps were to scale — 500 li (about 124 miles) to an inch. P'ei also included symbols to represent mountains, farm areas, boundaries of the capital city and the emperor's walled compound, roads, villages, and the borders of the various provinces. Names of the provinces were included, as well as those of cities, towns, and villages.

But the feature of these maps that made them unique was the overlay of a grid, comparable to latitude and longitude lines on modern maps. With the help of the grid lines it was possible to locate landscape features on the maps with considerable accuracy. By this single idea, P'ei had raised cartography to a highly technical level.

With the exception of an introduction P'ei wrote for his atlas, nothing remains of his work. Much of what we know of his cartographic skill comes from the writings of scholars of his period.

P'ei's idea of a map grid system was an important achievement. But he was not the first to think of it. The Greek astronomer and geographer Eratosthenes (circa 275–circa 195 B.C.) had already used a similar arrangement by dividing map surfaces into lines of latitude

and longitude. There is no evidence that P'ei Hsiu had
any knowledge of the Greek scholar's achievement.
Most historians feel the grid system for maps was
thought of separately by the two men, a common hap-
pening in the long history of science and technology.

Maps in ancient China were drawn on a variety of
materials, including wood. But silk was the most common. It was durable and pliable, so the maps were convenient to handle and carry. When a number of copies
of a map were desired, they were printed. The map was
cut into wood or stone. Ink was smeared on the surfaces of the materials and an imprint or block print was
made on the silk.

Following the invention of paper very early in
China's history, maps began to appear on this material.
Although paper was a great improvement, both for
printing and for drawing, it was fragile. Maps drawn
on paper in ancient China have long since disappeared.

The art of mapmaking, as well as the whole science
of geography, progressed steadily, if slowly, following
the significant contribution by P'ei Hsiu. This continued through the Sung Dynasty, established in A.D. 960,
a time when Chinese scholars reached golden heights
of achievement. The science of geography had its share
of great students during this period, led by two of the
more outstanding, Chia Tan and Chu Ssu-Pên.

It was during the late Sung Dynasty, in the twelfth
and thirteenth centuries, that China discarded much of
its land-oriented attitude and turned its attention to
maritime activities. The number of commercial and

naval ships expanded enormously. Some historians have estimated that China had the largest seagoing fleet of freighters and naval vessels in the world at this time.

Cargo-carrying junks sailed regularly to ports along China's coast, and in Korea, Japan, and the East Indies. A great number of them engaged in trade with Ceylon and India. Under Admiral Chêng Ho, Chinese fighting ships made long sea journeys to the West. Evidence of Chinese presence has been found on Africa's east coast and the Island of Madagascar, now the Malagasy Republic. All of this seagoing activity resulted in a great store of information for Chinese geographers.

Chinese geographers continued to become better informed about other lands during the sixteenth and seventeenth centuries. Compared with other centuries, this was a time when a veritable flood of visitors from different countries, especially from the West, came to China. Most important of these were Jesuit missionaries. They introduced a variety of intellectual attainments of Western scholarship in literature, the arts, and different fields of science, including geography.

The Jesuits brought the latest examples of the Western cartographers' work. For the most part these new maps were based on the startling discoveries of European navigators, who, in increasing numbers, were poking the bows of their caravels into the farthest corners of the earth.

As their awareness of the immensity and diversity of the world grew, Chinese geographers slowly gave up the old concept that their country was the center of the universe.

Biology

Scientists of ancient China were remarkably advanced in their knowledge of biology, the science of living things. Two factors were probably responsible for their great interest and achievements in this field. First was that agriculture was the chief activity of China's people. Even in the very early centuries efforts were made to improve plants and growing methods for larger harvests.

The second factor involved the use of plants to combat illness. Probably no other people in ancient times used so many different kinds of herbs and plants of the fields and forests for curing sickness and maintaining good health. Chinese botanical scholars were familiar with, and described in words and pictures, more than a thousand varieties of plants.

Because of the vast number of plants and their confusing characteristics, Chinese biologists were quick to realize that some form of classification would be helpful. Only by placing plants in an orderly arrangement would it be possible to study them with any measure of accuracy. They therefore established a system for cataloguing both plants and animals. It consisted of sixty-two divisions, in which the subjects were grouped in accordance with certain common characteristics.

The Chinese classification system anticipated a similar effort by Western scholars by some one thousand years. The famous Swedish botanist Carolus Linnaeus (1707–1778) was the originator of a plant and animal classification system that is still in use today with modifications. The botanical system devised by Linnaeus somewhat resembled the Chinese arrangement. It was based largely on certain characteristics of plants, such as the number of stamens and pistils in the flower.

Chinese biologists ranged widely in their studies. They made some of the earliest efforts at hybridizing plants and breeding animals for certain desired characteristics. One of their achievements in this field involved the breeding of goldfish for size and color. The fish were popular attractions in the garden pools of the nobility. The biologists also demonstrated their skill in a more practical way by developing improved rice plants. Chinese scientists were well advanced in hybridizing and breeding activities at the time of the Middle Ages in Europe.

Activity in the field of biology, botany particularly, was especially strong in the Sung Dynasty. This was a period in Chinese history when scholarly achievements were outstanding. A great number of written accounts on biological subjects appeared, principally on plants valued for their medicinal qualities. Many contained wood-block illustrations that were impressive both for their accuracy of detail and their beauty.

There is a strong belief among historians that the Chinese were the first to accompany the texts of books on medicinal plants with wood-block illustrations.

That idea may have worked its way west to Europe. A Chinese plant book that could have served as such an instructive agent was the *Chiu Husang Pên Tshao*, or *Famine Herbal*.

A book even more famous than this was written by one of the most versatile scholars of the Sung period, Shen Kua. It was encyclopedic in nature, containing many items on biology along with a number of other subjects. The book was called *Mêng Ch'i Pi Than*, or *Dream Pool Essays*, and is believed to have appeared in the late eleventh century.

The legacy of Chinese biologists of ancient times, in terms of their writings, leaves little doubt that they were the equal of the Greeks and certainly far ahead of their later European counterparts.

Geology

Geology is generally defined as the science dealing with the history of the earth as revealed in the physical structure of rocks. In their studies of this science Chinese scholars formulated some rather remarkable theories. One of these dealt with the formation of the earth. Very briefly, this theory maintained that when heavy matter in space solidified, rocks and the earth were created. A liquid also resulted from this cataclysmic action, forming the earth's seas and oceans. Wu Lin-Ch'uan (A.D. 1249–1333) was the source of this interesting theory.

Chinese geologists also gave a great deal of attention to the study of fossils. They knew that these solidified remains were once living animals and plants. This fact was not realized by European scientists until centuries later.

In dealing with the earth's rock formations on the surface, deep underground, and beneath the sea, Chinese scientists advanced many different views. But the one feature about rocks that held their special interest was the connection they had with earthquakes.

In China's long history the land has been wracked by numerous earthquakes, some of devastating proportions. One that was particularly catastrophic occurred in the late eighth century B.C. It has been recorded that the earth movement was so severe, the routes of three rivers were altered.

Because of their destructive characteristics, earthquakes have been studied and recorded in China since the earliest times. The noting of these events started even earlier than the date cited above and continued to the 1600s. Throughout this period almost a thousand earthquakes were listed. This record-keeping has become a great source of help to today's seismologists, geologists who are earthquake specialists. From a study of this centuries-long record, it has been concluded that major earthquakes occur in cycles, approximately every three decades.

Since earthquakes happened with considerable regularity over a long period of time, Chinese seismologists tried to develop a system for predicting them. The idea was quite modern. Seismologists today are striving to do much the same. But predicting exactly when an earthquake will occur has proved as difficult to present-day earth scientists as it was to early Chinese seismologists.

To balance their failure at predicting earthquakes Chinese seismologists were successful in another area of earthquake study. They developed the first practical seismograph, a device for registering the occurrence and severity of an earthquake at some distant point. The creation of this instrument preceded the construction of a similar device by Western scientists by some fifteen hundred years. The inventor of the world's first workable seismograph was Chang Hêng (A.D. 78–139), imperial astronomer at the emperor's court. A detailed description of this device will be given in a later section dealing with a host of Chinese inventions.

The science of geology has expanded into an enormously complex discipline since the studies of Chinese scholars in ancient times. It is to their credit, however, that they made the earliest and most significant advances in that field. If they had done nothing else but maintain a long record of earthquakes in their land and develop a seismograph, these accomplishments would have assured them a distinguished place in the historical development of geology.

Scientific matters were of great interest to Chinese scholars. Existing and newly discovered ancient writings and findings from archaeological diggings have amply confirmed that interest. As present-day scholarly research into China's past goes on at a faster pace than ever before, ancient Chinese scientific activities are coming to light. These, coupled with past findings, have increased greatly the admiration of the West for the wide range and modern character of the Chinese scientist's work.

4. Ancient Chinese Technology— Paper, Printing, Gunpowder, Compass

The ancient Chinese have been responsible for a remarkable number of inventions, many of great significance. Often, down through the centuries, the West has adopted the technical accomplishments of the Chinese with only the haziest idea of where they came from. It has been in comparatively modern times that the researches of scholars have made Western civilization aware of the rich legacy left by China's ancient technologists.

The list of Chinese inventions from ancient times is long. We do not intend to discuss all of these, only those of special importance, for example, paper, printing, gunpowder, and the compass. These have been singled out because, as one historian has observed, they have influenced the affairs of mankind as have no other technological creations.

Need was the single most important factor that accounted for the prolific outpouring of Chinese inventions. The old saying, Necessity is the mother of invention, seemed to be the credo of Chinese technologists. If a tool or mechanical apparatus was needed to help the farmer or weaver, the Chinese inventor went to work to make it. He was little interested in inventing for the sake of invention alone.

This was in contrast to the attitude of inventors in the West. For the most part, they invented for the pure love of tinkering and inventing. Once their technical creations were finished, a use for them was sought. Let us take a closer look at some of the handiwork of Chinese inventors.

Paper

Writing in ancient times was an extremely limited activity. Very few among the various peoples of the world had the knowledge or skill. Of course, there were mechanical reasons also for this limitation. For one, materials on which to write were few and crude.

In Sumeria, Babylon, Assyria, and other Middle Eastern countries, the use of cuneiform had developed. Cuneiform is a series of wedge-shaped characters made by pressing a stylus into the soft surface of a clay tablet. When the tablet was dried by the sun, the written message was permanently recorded. Thousands of these tablets have been unearthed by archaeologists and give us a fairly good idea of what those ancient civilizations were like.

Farther west, in Egypt, papyrus was being used as a writing material. It was made from the inner portion of a marsh reed. Papyrus provided an easier surface on which to write than clay and was surprisingly durable. It was used in Egypt for countless centuries. The Greeks and Romans also used papyrus extensively.

The Chinese had a well-developed system of writing as early as 1500 B.C. during the Shang Dynasty (circa 1766–1122 B.C.). Inscriptions of that period have been found on bronze bowls used for religious purposes, bronze weapons, pottery ware, and jade. The most common materials of this early period, however, were the scapulae — bones of animals and the shells of turtles. These were also vital for scapulimancy, one of the ancient Chinese practices for foretelling future events. Small indentations were cut into the bones or shells at particular spots. Heated stones or lengths of metal were then inserted in the depressions causing one or more cracks to appear. These were interpreted by a shaman to predict good or bad future happenings.

Gradually, other writing materials came into use — wood, bamboo, and silk. A sharp pointed knife was used if the message was to be inscribed on bone or metal; a simple brush and black ink if the writing surface was pottery ware, wood, or silk. Wood was preferred because of its availability. Bamboo was popular since its light weight made it fairly convenient to use more than one "page."

When prepared for writing purposes, bamboo stalks were cut into nine-inch lengths. These were just wide enough for a single column of written characters. It was because of this method of writing, within a narrow space, that Chinese writing became permanently fixed in a vertical rather than horizontal pattern as in the West.

Books were made of bamboo "pages." Holes were drilled in one end of a group of bamboo pages, which were then tied together with a leather thong or silk cord. A number of these bamboo books, among the earliest fashioned by man, have been found by archaeologists in Central Asia.

Obviously, bamboo books had their drawbacks, especially books having many pages. These were awkward to handle and carry. Many Chinese scholars, therefore, chose silk on which to inscribe their thoughts. Silk books were flexible, easily rolled, and could be carried around with little difficulty.

The main problem with silk, however, was its high cost and scarcity. There was little silk available as a writing material after its chief demand, for making clothing, was satisfied. There was a thriving market for this fine material not only in China but also in the West, to which it was exported in large quantities. The Romans, fond of luxuries, were particularly good customers of the silk merchants.

Almost everyone in ancient China who in one way or another engaged in writing — government officials, scholars, and professional scribes — eventually recognized the need for a better kind of writing material. Silk was scarce and not the easiest surface to write on. Wood and bamboo were cumbersome. When government reports had to be read by the governors of the provinces or even the emperor himself, they appeared to be hidden by a wood barrier.

The great inconvenience of these ancient writing materials called for something better — paper.

The invention of paper by the Chinese was an achievement of enormous importance. When it was invented, or by whom, is unknown. Some historians single out Ts'ai Lun as the inventor and A.D. 105 as the time when he produced the first crude paper material. But many other authorities disagree with this, pointing to ancient written records and archaeological findings that indicate paper was known and used long before Lun's time. Until more positive evidence is found we can only be certain that paper has a very old heritage indeed.

Whoever the inventor, the earliest form of paper was made from an unlikely collection of materials. These included worn-out fishnets cut into small pieces, old rags, the bark of trees, hemp, and various kinds of grasses. The materials were put into a large pot and boiled. The pulplike mass that resulted was removed, strained, and spread out to dry. A rough-surfaced paper was formed.

The new writing material caught on slowly but steadily. As scholars and professional scribes made increasing use of it, they found that paper was a good deal more convenient to use than the older materials. Paper took ink well and it was a lot easier to handle than wood or bamboo. Gradually these materials, along with silk, were discarded in favor of paper for writing purposes.

Like almost all inventions, the original paper was eventually improved upon. Over a period of time materials and methods for making paper underwent a change, and Chinese paper-makers were turning out a product of superior quality. Its fine, smooth surface and strength could not be excelled anywhere, even after the rest of the world had learned the secret of producing paper. Chinese paper manufacturers had discarded the original crude materials for their product and were substituting such items as rice flakes, algae from the sea, and the bark of the mulberry tree.

Papermakers at work

By the ninth century A.D. there were those in China who saw that paper could be used for many things besides writing. And so paper napkins were introduced, along with toilet tissue, paper money, and wallpaper. The latter was first made known to Europeans in the seventeenth century by Dutch traders who had come to China to exploit the vast new commercial opportunities that country presented. This brings up the matter of when paper-making was first introduced into Europe.

The story of paper's initial entrance into Europe is closely entwined with the history of the Arabs and the establishment of the enormous Islamic Empire. As Muhammad's religiously inspired legions swept out of the Arabian Peninsula and surged eastward, one country after another fell before their fierce attacks. By the eighth century they had overrun Turkestan, bordering China's western frontier. It was the Arabs' farthest eastward advance. The inhabitants of Turkestan were familiar with paper and the process for making it, having learned the art from the Chinese in the fifth century. The Arabs first encountered the product in July of 751 after capturing Turkestan's largest city, Samarkand.

The Arabs were quick to appreciate paper's value. Returning to the Middle East they lost little time erecting factories for its manufacture. The first of these appeared in Baghdad, in what is now Iraq, between 763 and 794. Others were established later in Damascus, in present-day Syria. In time, Damascus became the chief supplier of paper throughout the Western world.

In successive stages paper and the method for making it traveled ever farther westward. Following its introduction into Egypt, perhaps as early as the tenth century, paper soon displaced papyrus. A visitor to Cairo who later wrote of the sights in that bustling city was surprised to see merchants selling their wares wrapped in paper.

From Egypt paper continued to move west to Morocco, the westernmost outpost of the Islamic Empire. From here paper traveled north into Spain by A.D. 950. The Arabs controlled almost all of Spain for more than four centuries. It was during this period that paper made its earliest entry into Europe. However, Spain was not the only avenue by which this Chinese invention came. Paper also arrived via Constantinople, capital of the eastern half of the old Roman Empire, and through Sicily, still another part of the Arabs' empire. Paper was known and used in Sicily in 1109.

Spain was not only the first area in Europe to become aware of paper; it was also the scene for Europe's first paper-making industry. By 1150, Arabs and Spaniards were engaged in a flourishing paper-making business. Indeed, the quality and quantity of the paper made in Spain was so superior to the product made in Damascus that the industry in this Syrian city lost its monopoly after some five hundred years. Spain became the chief source of paper for much of Europe and the Middle East.

In 1276 the first paper mill was set up at Montefamo, Italy. The industry caught on quickly and by the early fourteenth century was thriving at such a pace that Spain was displaced as Europe's chief supplier of paper.

Paper of itself was unquestionably an important invention. But it had a far greater potential value, which few realized at the beginning of the material's existence. This was its union with printing, still some centuries away.

It is interesting, one might say almost a natural evolution, that the combining of paper and printing should also occur in China. Chinese technologists may well have been inspired in their development of printing by the existence of paper. In any case, when paper and printing were eventually brought together, the affairs of people throughout this world were to be profoundly altered.

Printing

Printing in ancient China came about slowly, over many centuries and after passing through a number of different stages. Before any mechanical method for duplicating writing came into existence, copies of written accounts — government decrees, scholarly reports, and religious messages of Buddhists, Taoists, and Confucians — had to be made by hand. It was a slow, laborious method. There was undoubtedly a great need for something better.

The technical road that led to printing began with seals and block printing. Much as today, seals were largely used on government documents. The practice began long before the Christian era and reached its peak during the former and later Han Dynasties (202 B.C.–A.D 220). The earliest seals were made with clay. First, an official symbol was inscribed on the surface of the soft clay. After the clay hardened, the surface was coated with red ink and then pressed onto the document. The impression left a white seal on a red background. Jade, gold, silver, copper, ivory, and rhinoceros horn were other materials used for making seals.

In a later variation of this method, the symbol was cut in relief. All the material surrounding it was removed so that the seal stood by itself. When it was covered with red ink and imprinted on the document, the seal came out red against a white background. This technique was destined to play an important role in the later stages of printing's advancement.

Buddhist monks were not always involved with quiet moments of prayer or meditation; they spent countless hours carving some of the basic beliefs of their religion onto stone slabs. Positioned around the grounds of the Buddhists' monasteries, the stone messages would serve to remind the monks of their calling. When visitors came to stroll through the grounds, they read and thought about the Buddhist beliefs. One of the most famous of these stone collections consists of more than seven thousand slabs carved between A.D. 600 and 1100.

Out of this Buddhist practice came the realization that if the stone messages were transferred to paper, copies could be made for many more readers. The result was a stone-rubbing technique, similar to the one in use today. Thin but strong paper was soaked in water and placed over the stone message, then firmly but carefully pressed into all the indentations with a stiff brush. After the paper dried, a swab of cotton was dipped into a container of black ink and spread over the paper. When the inked paper was removed from the stone slab, the message came out white on a black background. Stone rubbing became as popular among the Buddhist monks as their practice of cutting messages into stone.

It isn't known exactly when block printing was invented or who the inventor was. The best guess is that block printing originated around A.D. 600. This would put it in the T'ang Dynasty (A.D. 618–906), a time when Chinese intellectual and technical accomplishments were again at a peak. Available evidence tells us that block printing appears to have originated among the Buddhists.

Whatever the time or by whom invented, block printing was the final step before a method for printing itself was created. Early Chinese block printers would select a length of pear or jujube wood and cut it to a certain thickness and size. The surface was planed smooth and the block made exactly square. Then a paste of boiled rice was rubbed into the block to give the surface greater smoothness. This also softened the wood somewhat so that the characters or illustration could be cut into it more easily.

While the block was being prepared, skilled scribes transferred the text to be printed onto very thin, transparent paper. Two pages of this paper were carefully laid onto the surface of the block, which was coated with a sticky substance. The pages were put down so that the text was in reverse.

After drying and becoming firmly attached to the block, the paper was rubbed off. The process left the written characters imprinted on the block. The block carver now took over, cutting away all of the surface material around each of the characters. When the carving was completed, all the characters were left standing in relief. The block was now ready to be used for printing.

Black ink was spread over the characters or illustration to be printed. Paper was laid over the block and carefully but firmly smoothed out with a brush. The result was a clear print of the original. This could be duplicated any number of times. Essentially, this was the technique Chinese block printers followed for centuries. They became extraordinarily skilled at the art and turned out work of unsurpassed quality. This was especially true of their illustrations.

Block printing caught on quickly in ancient China, and printed matter — books and pamphlets — increased in numbers. One of the most remarkable achievements of Chinese block printers was a monumental Buddhist religious writing, the *Tripitaka*. Translated from the Sanskrit into Chinese, the *Tripitaka* was a collection of Buddhist beliefs. It consisted of more than five thousand volumes and 130,000 pages. This meant that the printers had to cut 130,000 wood blocks, one for each page, a stupendous job. The project, carried out in the Sung Dynasty, was begun in A.D. 972 and completed in 983.

Despite its huge size, the *Tripitaka* was revised and reprinted a number of times. One of the revised copies was brought to Japan some time between 1469 and 1486. All but two volumes of this copy still exist. An older companion book to the *Tripitaka* is the *Diamond Sutra*, another volume of Buddhist scriptures. Printed in A.D. 868, it is considered the oldest existing example of ancient Chinese block printing.

When first invented, block printing was devoted almost entirely to religious subjects. In time this changed, so that by the 1300s Chinese printers were turning out a variety of products. Perhaps the most interesting of the nonreligious items was paper money, the first to be made and used, early in the eleventh century, by any people in the world. Paper money was widely circulated in ancient China, but before its creation iron currency was the common medium of exchange. It so happened that this metal currency became exhausted following an uprising of the people in Szechuan Province, creating chaos in government affairs. To help re-establish a money supply, some government official got the idea of using paper currency.

Probably because of its novelty or convenience when carried and used, paper money was readily accepted by the people. The paper used for money was gray in color and imprinted with an official government symbol made from a copper seal. The size of the paper money when it first appeared generally depended on the amount of currency it represented. Some of it was extremely large.

Red-and-black paper money as big as a sheet of typewriter paper appeared in the fifteenth century A.D., during the Ming Dynasty. Some of the bills still exist, and collectors of old paper money, like stamp hobbyists, will pay several thousand dollars for a good specimen.

Since the Chinese were the first to print and use paper money, they were also the first to learn of its negative aspects — forgery and inflation. Forgery was really not a major problem, since those caught making illegal money were quickly put to death. This was enough to discourage most would-be forgers. Inflation was a much more serious matter.

Inflation, with its cheapening of currency, was one of the chief causes of the downfall of the Sung Dynasty. An observer of that period wrote that as the prices of goods rose, the value of paper money fell correspondingly. He went on to say that this state of affairs destroyed the people's incentive to work. He might well have been writing about the present economic affairs of many countries.

Europeans may have first learned about printing through paper money. In the late thirteenth century this type of currency was being printed not only in China but also in Tabriz, in present-day Iran. Marco

Polo spent twenty years in China. Writing of his travels after returning to Italy, he told of many new and strange things he had seen, including paper money. Of this he said, ". . . and the Kaan causes every year to be made such a vast quantity of this money [paper] which costs him nothing that it must equal all the treasure in the world." Playing cards — sheet-dice, as the Chinese called them — were another early printed item that was introduced into Europe and became enormously popular.

The westward movement of block printing from China involved many peoples and political developments. The Turks played a leading role in the course of their migrations from Central Asia to the Middle East. The Mongols and their vast conquests through all of Asia, Russia, and the eastern part of Europe were an even greater factor in bringing block printing to the West.

By the twelfth and thirteenth centuries, Europeans were fully engaged in block printing. Germany, Italy, and Holland had quickly developed into the most important centers of the printing art.

Traveling eastward, to Korea and Japan, block printing reached those countries by the tenth century. Printers there were as skilled as their counterparts in China. It is believed that the oldest examples of block printing for which there are positive dates are those of Japanese make.

Chinese technologists were not content with block printing. There were some who felt the method had room for improvement. It was almost as slow, for example, as the handwritten technique for making duplicate copies. Pi Shêng was one such technical-minded individual who believed printing could be made better, at least faster. Working some time between 1041 and 1048, Pi Shêng developed a printing method that used a number of pieces of type fixed to a square metal plate and locked together by a frame. Each piece of type, representing a character to be printed, was made out of clay, then baked and hardened.

The surface of the square iron plate was covered with a glue made of pine resin, wax, and paper ashes. An iron frame was placed around the plate, forming a low-sided box. The hardened clay type was arranged within the frame to form a solid pattern of type. A wooden board was then placed over all and pressed firmly downward. This made the type even.

After the top surfaces of the type were coated with ink, paper was laid over the frame and carefully pressed. Pi Shêng's printing method used two type forms. While one was being employed for printing, a second was prepared with fresh type. The movable type and dual forms did speed up the art of printing, as Pi Shêng had confidently believed.

The real importance of Pi Shêng's contribution to printing, however, was the unique arrangement of type. The many pieces he used and locked firmly together formed, in a sense, a single large block for printing. This elementary system of typesetting was to be a key factor in the later and still more advanced development in printing that occurred in the West.

Johann Gutenberg (circa 1397–1468) of Germany is generally considered in the West to be the inventor of movable-type printing. His chief contributions were the use of metal molds for making type and a mechanical pressing action for printing. Metal molds, however, were not his exclusive idea, as we have seen. These were used in China and Korea centuries before Gutenberg employed them.

Chinese achievements in the development of an efficient printing process may have influenced Johann Gutenberg's work. We do not know. What is more certain is that with the invention of printing, pamphlets, books, and all sorts of printed matter became vastly more numerous. The common people's desire and ability to read were greatly stimulated. New ideas were freely exchanged. This development over a period of time set in motion great currents of social upheaval. In Europe particularly, printing contributed to bringing about the Renaissance.

Gunpowder

Of the many things that filled Marco Polo with wonder during his twenty years of traveling around China, one of the most astonishing was gunpowder. He wrote that the noise of its explosion was so loud, the listener wanted to plug his ears and throw his cloak over his head.

By the time Marco Polo heard his first explosive

bang, shortly after 1275, gunpowder had been greatly improved over its earliest form. Like most of China's ancient technical accomplishments, next to nothing is known about its origin. It may well have its roots in the form of firecrackers used to celebrate religious festivals and the dawn of a new year.

However, these first firecrackers were not man-made. They were short lengths of bamboo that exploded when thrown into a fire. Alchemists may have gotten the idea for man-made explosives from these noisemakers. They were long familiar with mixing all sorts of natural and mineral substances and could have stumbled on the formula for gunpowder.

By the eleventh century gunpowder, *huo yao*, or "fire drug," was in common use in China. And since warfare was almost a way of life in ancient China — internal fights or defensive battles with Mongol invaders — it was a simple process to employ gunpowder on the battlefield. It was through its military use that we have one of the earliest written accounts about gunpowder. This was a military manual written by Wu Ching Tsung Yao in A.D. 1044.

According to the manual, gunpowder was a mixture of saltpeter (potassium nitrate), charcoal, and sulfur, each in certain proportions. Saltpeter was in the largest component. The substance was dangerous to work with because it could easily be ignited by accident. Therefore a word of caution was given to makers of gunpowder so that they would not suffer "singed beards" or have their workshops burned to the ground.

The ingredients of gunpowder were no mystery to Chinese alchemists. They had known about saltpeter and sulfur for almost a millennium. Both had been commonly used for medicinal purposes. The secret was to combine them with other ingredients in the right amounts to make the mixture explode when ignited.

Wu Ching Tsung Yao's manual also gave directions for making a bomb using gunpowder. A paste of dried leaves, tung oil, and wax was added to the explosive mixture of saltpeter, sulfur, and charcoal and thoroughly combined. Finally, all of this was wrapped in several layers of paper and tied securely with rope. Then the incendiary bundle, or bomb, was coated with pitch and wax.

Bombs or grenades such as this may have been used in warfare as early as A.D. 1000, when troops of the Sung Empire were locked in desperate combat with the Liao Tartars. An account of the struggle described how grenades were used by the Sung forces against the enemy. These were thrown by hand or lobbed by catapult among the attackers. Before each bomb was thrown, a fuse attached to it was ignited.

The grenades were effective, especially against troops who had never experienced them before. Noting this, Chinese military technologists proceeded to create a whole family of weapons. One with a particularly modern touch was called a flame thrower. The weapon consisted of a container of oil and gunpowder. When it was ignited, a tongue of fire shot through an attached bamboo tube for several feet and out the front end.

The flame-throwing weapon was already in use about the time the primitive grenade was being made. Some one thousand years later, in World War II, the flame thrower was resurrected, modernized, and converted into a far more diabolical fighting tool.

A less complicated but equally deadly weapon developed by ancient Chinese military technicians may have been the ancestor of today's rifle and cannon. This was a bamboo tube about two feet long that shot stone or iron pellets out the front end. A charge of gunpowder and an igniting fuse were at the other end. The tube was tightly bound with string to keep it from splitting or blowing apart after the charge went off. Tubes were also made of several wrappings of paper glued together.

Instead of discharging pellets from a tube, soldiers would sometimes fire a single large projectile. This was the beginning of the cannon, which the Chinese may have used in the middle of the thirteenth century. Since Chinese technologists were highly skilled at casting iron and bronze by this time, it was an easy step for them to consider making metal cannon barrels. As a result, bronze cannon were common by the early fourteenth century. This put the Chinese a good half-century ahead of Europeans in the manufacture of cannon. A Chinese bronze cannon of the fourteenth century still survives in a Peking museum. The ancient weapon is fourteen inches long and weighs about sixteen pounds. By today's standards it would be considered no more than a toy.

Of all the gunpowder weapons developed by ancient

Chinese technologists, the one of most interest to many of us today is the rocket. A primitive device to be sure, the rocket nevertheless operated on the same basic principles as modern rockets. The weapon consisted of an arrow with a short length of bamboo fixed to its shaft. The tube was tightly packed with gunpowder. A fuse extended from one end of the tube; the other end was blocked up. Ignited by the fuse, the gunpowder blasted rearward, sending a flame-tipped arrow on a soaring flight against enemy soldiers.

Rocket arrows were used in A.D. 1126 by the defenders of Kaifeng, capital of the Sung Empire. The city was under powerful attack by the Liao Tartars, who had swept down from the plains of Mongolia and had seized nearly all of the northern provinces. The capture of Kaifeng would put them in complete control of the empire. Although the rocket arrows used by the defenders took their toll, the weapon was not enough to prevent the capital's seizure by the enemy.

The rocket arrow of ancient China is of interest because it was the crude forerunner of the mighty rockets of the present age. Some nine hundred years later, enormously powerful rocket vehicles were built that permitted man to travel through space and to walk on the surface of the moon.

After the thirteenth century, Chinese technologists did little to improve the explosive force of gunpowder or its use in weaponry. One reason for this, perhaps, was that incessant warfare had died down, now that the Tartars were in control of the land. There was little need for new weapons.

Rocket arrows and launching box

This was in direct contrast to the attitude in the West, Europe in particular, once the secret of making gunpowder became known there. Roger Bacon (circa 1214–1294), an English scientist and philosopher, was the first to mention it, along with a formula for producing it, in one of his many treatises. How he learned about it is far from clear; perhaps he read about gunpowder in Arab literature. Arabs had become acquainted with gunpowder in the course of their trading activities with the Chinese. Some scholars say that German alchemists may have discovered the formula for making gunpowder on their own.

By the fourteenth century, gunpowder was being made by Europeans on a relatively large scale. They were quick to see that it was extremely useful in warfare. Weapons could be made that were many times more destructive and deadly than any existing before. Rifles, hand guns, and cannon became common, and it wasn't long before lances and crossbows were turned into museum pieces.

When the Portuguese navigator Fernão Pérez sailed his fleet of caravels into Canton harbor in 1514, the first European ships to enter Chinese waters, he announced his arrival with a salvo from his cannon. The Chinese were astonished at the loud noise and large size of the cannon. Nothing like them existed in their country. It was not until modern times that Chinese technologists made similar large weapons.

Compass

Curiosity about the magnetic quality of lodestone led the technologists of ancient China to invent the compass. The story of this direction-pointing device begins at a very early time in China's history and covers many stages.

One Chinese legend, over two thousand years old, is credited with the first reference to a direction-pointing device. It is a tale about the Yellow Emperor's South-Pointing Carriage. In ancient China yellow was the color associated with royalty.

The carriage was a two-wheeled vehicle the emperor used for traveling around his realm. The wheels were hooked up to other wheels, or gears, by driving belts. An arm, extending from the carriage, was ingeniously connected to the gearing. No matter in what direction the carriage was headed, the extended arm always pointed to the south.

To the ancient Chinese, the south point of the compass was important, not the north. The south had a symbolic significance associated with the well-being of the emperor. A carriage similar to the Yellow Emperor's was built by a brilliant mathematician and engineer, Tsu Ch'ung-chih, late in the fifth century A.D. He was curious to know whether such a carriage would actually work. To his surprise, it did.

An early development that had more to do with the creation of an actual compass was a south-pointing fish-shaped device. It was described in a Chinese military manual by Tsêng Kung-Liang in A.D. 1044. The fish for this primitive compass was made from a thin strip of iron, two inches long by one-half inch wide. Heated to a red-hot state, it was carefully removed from the fire with its tail pointing north and its head south, following the line of the earth's magnetic field. Kept in this position, the fish pointer was doused in cold water and became magnetized. When the pointer was floated in a basin of water, the head of the fish pointed continuously to the south. It is not known if the device was ever put to use.

Another early compass development made use of a diviner's board. This was a basic tool of geomancers, who practiced the art of foretelling the future. The diviner's board, or *shih*, was a wooden square with a bronze circular plate in the center. The square shape represented the ancient Chinese conception of the earth. Magic symbols, constellations of the stars, and the four cardinal points of the compass were painted on the surface of the square board. The bronze circular plate represented the heavens or space curving around the earth. It was mounted on a pivot and turned. Its surface was decorated with twenty-four constellations, with the seven main stars of the Great Bear occupying the center of this cluster.

The geomancer operated the *shih* by spinning the bronze plate. When it stopped, the tail of the bear would point to one of the symbols or constellations on the square board. At this point, the geomancer would proceed to recite pleasant or unpleasant future happenings for his client.

All of this may seem to have little to do with a compass. Nevertheless, at some point during the Han Dynasty, well after 200 B.C., an imaginative technologist saw another use for the *shih*. The circular bronze plate was removed, and a spoon made of lodestone was put in its place. The surface of the diviner's board was highly polished. After the spoon was spun and came to a stop, it was supposed to rest in a line with the earth's magnetic field, pointing north and south. The device was interesting only as an experiment. It wasn't practical mainly because the spoon proved erratic about stopping in a north-south direction.

Ancient Chinese technologists went on to develop still another compass, one that showed the first real signs of usefulness. It consisted of a short length of wood carved in the form of a fish. A piece of lodestone was embedded in its belly. The crude compass needle

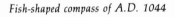

Fish-shaped compass of A.D. 1044

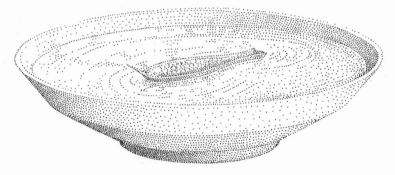

was then placed in a bowl of water. Picking up the earth's magnetic field, the compass needle floated in a north-south direction. This invention is generally pointed to as the first practical liquid compass and appears to have been in existence since A.D. 1100.

A crude type of the so-called dry compass was developed after the liquid model. It was simple in construction, consisting of a magnetized steel needle tied to a length of silk thread. This was suspended above a board on which the major compass points had been marked. Once it stopped turning on the slender thread, the needle pointed in a north-south direction.

This type of compass proved unsatisfactory. The needle took too long to stop twisting around on the thread to provide a quick reading, and it was easily disturbed by vibrations. As a device for direction-pointing the liquid compass was the first to be made use of by the Chinese. Its most important application was to help sailors find their way at sea. Chinese seamen were using the liquid compass for navigation as early as the eleventh century. On the heavily traveled trade routes to Korea and the East Indies, Chinese mariners guided themselves with the help of the stars, chiefly the North Star. The sun was another helpful beacon. When the weather turned cloudy and stormy, the compass and its south-pointing needle was used. Geomancers, land surveyors, and astronomers were others who found the liquid compass helpful in their activities.

Westerners probably found out about the compass

near the end of the twelfth century; some of their earliest writings on this device appeared about this time. And, as with so many ancient Chinese inventions, it was the Arabs who brought the compass to the attention of the West.

When knowledge of the compass reached Italy, its value was quickly appreciated by the navigators of that country. Ideas for improving the Chinese liquid type were soon being explored. Out of this activity came the well-known compass card — Rose Ventorum, or "wind rose." This was an elaborate presentation of the compass points on the surface of a square or circular card. A magnetic compass needle was mounted in the center on a pivot. The Italian version of the compass was a big improvement over the liquid type. When it reached China in the sixteenth century, the Rose compass soon displaced the earlier Chinese model for shipboard use.

The invention and application of the compass for navigation at sea was about as revolutionary in its impact on the West, Europe particularly, as gunpowder. European mariners roamed the farthest reaches of the earth, discovering new lands and peoples. Through the successes of seamen, which the compass made possible, European rulers acquired vast empires and unsurpassed wealth. At the same time, these achievements made the world a much smaller place. Remote and often isolated peoples were brought into the mainstream of human activity, not always, sadly enough, to their advantage or benefit.

5. *Inventions, Inventions, Inventions*

The horse was domesticated about three thousand years before the Christian era. The Chinese, along with their neighbors in Central Asia, were among the earliest of the ancient peoples to put the animal to work. Europeans followed approximately a thousand years later. In both parts of the world, the horse's strength, stamina, and speed were quickly made use of for a variety of chores that man himself did either poorly or not at all. The most common tasks given the horse were those where pulling was required — helping with plowing, for example, and drawing carts and carriages.

To perform its pulling jobs, the horse needed some kind of harness arrangement. The equipment created by Europeans worked but was inefficient and harmful to the animal. It was rigged in such a manner that the beast could not apply its full strength. The harness encircled the horse's neck and partly choked the creature. As a consequence, only about 50 percent of its pulling power was utilized.

The Chinese developed a harness that was much superior. It was arranged so that when the horse pulled, pressure was concentrated across the animal's chest, not around its neck. Illustrations from as early as the second century A.D. show this harness. However, the harness may have been developed and used a thousand years earlier.

At some period in the sixth century, the Chinese version of an equine harness was introduced into Europe. It may have come by way of the Slavs and eastern Germans. Since the horse could work so much more comfortably and efficiently with the Chinese harness, it replaced the European type in a relatively short time.

Riding a horse bareback while holding on to its mane was probably the earliest mode of using the creature for transportation. It is more than likely that this would have come long before the animal was trained to pull wagons or carriages. But it was an uncomfortable way of riding, and tugging the horse's mane was a nearly impossible way to control its actions. In due time the ingenuity of man provided a bit, bridle, and saddle to improve matters. But one item was still missing to complete the rider's comfort and to put the animal under his full control — the stirrup.

The origin of the stirrup is unclear, but the earliest reference to it appears in a Chinese account, dating from about A.D. 477, of the horse's use in military combat. The stirrup was mentioned at the time by a Chinese military officer writing about his years of service in the emperor's army. Difficult as it is to pin down historically, scholars feel certain that the stirrup was known and used before the fifth century, not only in China but also in Korea. Following that period, it was widely employed, particularly by mounted troops throughout the Far East.

The stirrup helped the rider of the horse in that it increased his stability and control of the animal. By pressing his knees and lower legs against the horse's sides, the rider was able to make the horse respond to commands. This was especially important for the mounted soldier, since the stirrup allowed him to free his hands for better handling of weapons, such as the lance and crossbow. The latter was especially difficult to use while riding a horse, since it required both hands.

As time passed, knowledge of the stirrup made its way slowly westward, to the peoples of the steppes of southern Russia, the inhabitants of the Danube region, and eventually the Balkan Peninsula. It was along this avenue at some unknown period that the stirrup entered western Europe.

As inventions go, the wheelbarrow would hardly seem a technical creation of any importance. Yet as humble a contrivance as it may be, the wheelbarrow has proved extremely helpful through the long years of its existence. Chuko Liang (A.D. 181–234), a general at the time of China's Three Kingdoms, is usually considered the wheelbarrow's inventor.

The earliest wheelbarrows were not quite like those used today. The single wheel was in the middle of the

An early wheelbarrow

rolling unit, not at the front end. Nevertheless, it was moved by a single individual, like the existing types. At some later period the wheel was shifted to the front end of the shafts.

Prior to the invention of the wheelbarrow there was a similar device without a wheel. It was more like a litter that was carried by two men, one at either end. For countless ages it was a common carrier of people, building materials, and farm products. The addition of a wheel greatly improved the transport. It not only made moving people and things a good deal easier; the vehicle also saved labor because only one man was needed to operate it.

In addition to its employment for transporting people, agricultural products, and materials for construction projects, the wheelbarrow was highly useful in warfare. Soldiers transported supplies with it and removed the wounded and dead from the battlefield.

Europeans first became familiar with the wheelbarrow in the twelfth or thirteenth century, more than a thousand years after its invention. One historian has observed that it came along at just the right moment to be an invaluable aid in the construction of Europe's magnificent cathedrals.

The wheelbarrow went through another phase of development at the hands of Chinese technicians when they added masts and sails to the transport. Wind-filled sails were considered helpful for propelling heavily loaded wheelbarrows. The concept didn't last very long, but it may have been the stimulus that led Simon Stevin (1548–1620), a Dutch physicist and engineer, to experiment with a similar transport. He built four-wheeled carriages equipped with masts and sails. Stevin sailed these along the beaches of Holland and demonstrated that they could transport people at a top speed of close to forty miles per hour. Although Stevin's wind-driven carriages were no more permanent than those of the Chinese, his experiments produced one positive result. They showed that the human body could tolerate high speed, something that European scientists had not believed.

Throughout its long history, the kite has served as a useful tool and a pleasure-giving toy. The earliest definite reference to it in China, home of its origin, dates back to A.D. 549. A historical account tells about the siege of the capital city of T'ai-Ch'êng (Nanking) and the emperor trapped within its walls. In an effort to tell his friends and allies outside the city's bounds that he was well, the emperor ordered a kite with a message attached flown above the compound. When the attackers saw the bobbing, airborne object, sharpshooting bowmen tried knocking it down. We are not sure if they succeeded, but the attempt may possibly be considered, as one scholar has observed, the first demonstration of antiaircraft fire in battle.

How or when the kite was created is a mystery, but there are many legends available to substitute for fact. One story tells of farmers who, in the heat of summer, worked in the fields wearing lightweight straw hats. If the hats were not securely tied, the wind would often blow them off. This happened frequently to one farmer, who eventually got tired of chasing and retrieving his hat. He decided to do something about it, and tied a long string to the brim. From then on, when the wind blew and his hat sailed away on a current of air, the farmer would simply haul it in with the string. Perhaps this farmer or another who watched him thought it great fun to hold on to an object tossing to and fro on the wind — and the kite was born.

The kite's dual nature, as a toy and as a utilitarian device, probably developed at about the same time. Children in ancient times took to it quickly and, like children today, delighted in holding on to the tugging, wind-tossed kite. Kites for work or play in ancient China were made of wood, paper, or silk. With their usual originality, the Chinese often made kites to represent all sort of fanciful creatures.

There were a number of practical uses for the fragile object, the most common, perhaps, in warfare. During a battle, one side or the other would fly kites carrying messages urging surrender. Fishermen would frequently use kites to carry bait to some distant, desirable fishing spot. Engineers building bridges found the kite of great help for transporting lines over river gorges.

From China the kite became known to the Koreans, Japanese, and the peoples of other lands of the Far East. Wherever it appeared the kite was received with enthusiasm. Knowledge about the kite traveled west via the Muslim world. Arabs and others of the Islamic Empire were flying kites in the seventh century. In the late 1500s the kite was introduced into Europe by way of the Italians, who were the first to fly it. Not long afterward, English children and adults were enjoying the diving, swooping kite.

When it first appeared in Europe the kite was looked on mainly as a toy. But eventually, as in China, inventive minds found practical uses for it. And so the kite was employed at shore-based rescue stations to fly lifelines to ships wrecked on the shore. It was used for carrying weather-recording instruments to high altitudes. One of its more practical applications was as a research tool. It was through flying a kite in Colonial America during a thunderstorm that Benjamin Franklin, a man of many talents, proved that lightning was an electric discharge.

In 1822 an Englishman, George Pocock, hooked up a series of kites to pull a stagecoach. The government thought so well of his idea that it granted him a patent in 1826. If the current oil problem in the United States and elsewhere intensifies, Pocock's idea as an energy substitution for transport may well be revived!

Perhaps the kite's greatest involvement with research was the help it provided in making possible flight by heavier-than-air objects. The sleek commercial jet airliners streaking through the skies today actually owe their existence to kites. Early aeronautical pioneers like Alexander Graham Bell and the Wright brothers flew wing-shaped kites to study their lifting power.

The kite ranks among the oldest of the creations by technologists of China. Enduring for almost two thousand years, it has brought delight to children and adults the world over. Not many of man's technical achievements can claim a similar distinction.

Some six centuries before Europeans first developed clockwork mechanisms, especially the metal escapement part, Chinese technicians had made enormous strides in the field. Chinese mechanical clocks were already in common use between A.D. 700 and 1300. It was only after the latter date that Europeans were employing similar timekeeping devices. Chinese clockwork achievements have been described as the "missing link" between the very old water clocks (clepsydras) of Babylon and Egypt and the purely mechanical clocks of modern times.

As noted earlier, Chinese astronomers used clockwork mechanisms to build moving observational equipment. Their supreme effort was the great astronomical clock constructed on the grounds of the Imperial Palace at Kaifeng in 1088–1092.

In nineteenth-century Europe a similar clockwork mechanism was invented by the German astronomer Joseph von Fraunhofer, in 1842. His device was linked to a telescope so that the latter could track the movement of stars. Although the Chinese had built their unit almost eight hundred years earlier, Fraunhofer is credited with having achieved his invention quite independently.

Earlier mention was made of the surprising amount of knowledge scientists of ancient China had regarding earthquakes. The fact that China through the ages has been the scene of countless numbers of these destructive events has made that study almost imperative. The seismograph was an important tool that helped Chinese scientists in this work. The device they designed and built for detecting earthquakes was the first of its kind.

Chang Hêng, the eminent astronomer of the Imperial Chancellory for Astronomical and Calendrical Science who made the first practical seismograph, was more than a scientist. He was also a skilled engineer, inventor, and mathematician. Writing poetry and painting were his favorite ways of relaxing.

In the study of earthquakes, Chang Hêng and his scientific colleagues felt handicapped by receiving information about earth tremors weeks after they occurred at some distant part of the country. They desired more immediate data. Chang Hêng was one of several scientists who put their minds to the problem and came up with the world's first earthquake alarm. The device was capable of recording quakes and of indicating approximately the distance of the event and its location.

Chang Hêng's seismograph looked and operated like a toy rather than a scientific instrument. It was a large unit made in the form of a copper kettle about six feet in diameter. The sensitive mechanism that signaled a quake was inside the kettle. Eight dragon heads were fixed at regular intervals around the upper rim of the kettle. Each of these had movable jaws in which a metal ball was placed. Eight bronze toads were set around the bottom of the kettle. These were positioned directly below the heads of the dragons in a sitting position, heads raised and mouths wide open.

When an earthquake occurred and the resulting shock wave struck the kettle, the dragon facing in the direction from which the wave came would open its mouth and release the metal ball. Falling straight down, the ball would land in the waiting mouth of a toad. At this point a bell would also ring, alerting an observer, and the dragon's jaws would snap shut. The device was a source of endless wonder to all who saw it in action.

In the summer of 1980 the People's Republic of China held an exhibit of crafts and industrial products in San Francisco, California. A highlight of the show was a model of Chang Hêng's ancient seismograph.

For countless ages the Chinese were primarily a land-oriented people. They were little interested in the world beyond their borders. As the centuries passed, this attitude changed, and they became deeply involved with affairs of the sea. Voyages of exploration were undertaken; commercial links were established with far-off countries; and fishing became a vigorous industry to help feed a rapidly growing population. In addition, China's naval forces increased greatly. By the thirteenth century its warships had grown to twenty squadrons, manned by more than fifty thousand seamen. At this time, and for a considerable period thereafter, China had more ships afloat than any other country in the world. Fundamental to all its maritime activities were seaworthy vessels. And these the Chinese had. Their shipbuilders had learned their trade well, designing and building ships that were superior to any then sailing the seas.

No one knows for certain the origin of the term "junk," commonly used to identify the Chinese ship. One thing is sure: it has no relation to the usual meaning of that word. It is difficult to make a comparison between the junk and a Western ship. How its design came to be is unknown. Naval historians are agreed, however, that it was no overnight creation. It evolved to its ultimate form only after the passage of many centuries.

The Chinese junk is built without a keel, which is the backbone of Western ships. It has a flat-bottomed hull and a blunt bow and stern. These hull features appear to have been based on bamboo rafts, simple craft used in a limited way in coastwise shipping more than three thousand years ago. The unique part of the Chinese junk is its interior hull. This is divided into a number of small watertight compartments, strengthened with transverse bulkheads. This feature of shipbuilding was unknown to naval architects of the West until the last decades of the eighteenth century. The separate compartments within the hull greatly increased the ship's safety margin. If the hull was accidentally stove in by a submerged rock or by a collision with another vessel, only part of the hull would become flooded rather than the entire interior, as would be the case with a Western ship. This compartment feature was adopted by Western shipbuilders only after much urging by those who clearly saw that it would add greatly to the safety of sailing vessels.

Benjamin Franklin in 1787 wrote in praise of the Chinese method of using watertight compartments for ship construction. He was especially enthusiastic about incorporating this feature on the fast packet ships carrying mail and passengers between England and America. Knowing that the vessel was built with this safety feature, he said, would be a great encouragement to the passengers.

The watertight compartments of the Chinese junk led to a practice that influenced Western maritime activities centuries later. Seamen aboard junks would often flood the forward compartment, letting sea water come in through special holes in the bow. It was com-

mon with junks sailing the inland rivers where dangerous rapids were encountered. The added weight in the
bow made it possible for the sailors to control the vessel in the powerful river currents. The wild up-and-
down tossing of the boat could be reduced. The com-
partment-flooding technique was also practiced by
fishermen. They would throw their fish catch into the
flooded compartment to keep it fresh until they
reached shore. English fishermen, who seem to have
discovered the practice on their own, did the same
thing with their catches in the 1700s.

The Chinese practice of flooding a compartment led
to still another maritime development in the West:
water ballast for improving the equilibrium of a ship. A
ship that was scheduled to return home empty after de-
livery of a cargo would often have its hold partly filled
with water for ballast. Rocks would sometimes be substituted. The added weight allowed the ship to sail better, especially through heavy seas. This made it easier
for the helmsman to guide his vessel.

Finally, the Chinese flooded-compartment idea may
have had its most important influence of all in the West
with the invention and development of the submarine.
These undersea vessels can dive and rise in the ocean
waters only by means of flooded and emptied compartments built into the sides of the hull.

The sternpost rudder was almost as important as the
compass for making possible the Great Age of Exploration by Western navigators. The sternpost, vital
for steering and controlling a ship, was already in use

on Chinese junks in the first century B.C. Early ships in the West, lacking this feature, were controlled by a long oar, sometimes two, extending from the stern. The oar was manipulated by a steersman, who, by pushing it to the right or left, made the vessel go in either of those directions. The Vikings' graceful longboat often had a steersman at the bow as well as the stern. The long oar for steering served well enough while boats sailed on inland waters or along a coast. For ocean voyages the long oar was not effective. The sternpost rudder first became known to European shipbuilders about 1180. However, more than a century passed before they incorporated the Chinese invention on oceangoing caravels and galleons.

Shipbuilders of ancient China also developed the balanced rudder and the fenestrated rudder in the eleventh century. The latter had a series of holes through its surface. These were found to make steering easier by reducing pressure against the rudder. The balanced rudder was adopted by Western naval architects in the middle of the nineteenth century and the fenestrated rudder at the beginning of the twentieth century.

Chinese junks were built in different sizes, depending on where they were to be used — lakes, bays, rivers, or the open seas. Oceangoing junks were surprisingly large. A number of them weighed as much as fifteen hundred tons and were up to two hundred feet in length. They were manned by crews of several hundred.

Junks were built mostly of fir and pine. Outer hulls

were a single layer, when the ship was first constructed, and were tightly caulked. However, when the vessel was overhauled, a second layer of wood was simply added onto the first and the seams again caulked. Chinese shipbuilders were carrying on this practice as early as the eleventh century. Europeans did not follow suit until more than five centuries later.

The battle between the *Monitor* and the *Merrimack* in the American Civil War was the first encounter between ironclad vessels, which, according to most Western naval historians, made their appearance only a few years before. The Chinese, however, could cite the existence of metal-clad ships in their country as far back as the twelfth century. These were naval vessels whose upper decks and hulls were covered with metal.

Living quarters for crew and passengers aboard the junks were generally built abovedeck. The larger vessels had as many as sixty cabins. Merchants traveling to distant overseas markets made up the bulk of the passengers. They would often bring their families along, cooking and eating in their cabins. Sea voyages were long, so passengers and crew would bring aboard buckets for growing favorite herbs and vegetables.

Chinese junks, especially the oceangoing types, usually had more than one mast. Sometimes as many as five would be erected on a ship. Multiple masts in ancient times were unusual, yet the Chinese were using them in the third century, long before the West. When Chinese shipbuilders installed masts they did not place them in a straight line. Rather, the masts were slightly

Ocean-going junk

staggered. The builders believed that the sails would catch the wind better with this arrangement. When Western shipbuilders began installing more than one mast on their vessels in the fifteenth century, they preferred keeping them in a straight line. The staggered method of the Chinese was never adopted, perhaps because of the way the masts were secured below deck. They were firmly anchored to the keel, which had to be exactly straight.

Although cloth was sometimes used for sails on Chinese junks, bamboo was more common. Strips of bamboo were made into flexible mats. These were hoisted and lowered much as one raises and lowers a venetian blind. The sails had a limited turning movement right and left around the masts. This enabled the crew to turn them so that they could receive the wind to the best advantage. The sail arrangement of Chinese junks permitted them to sail with a quartering wind and even to windward more efficiently than the ships of the West.

The Chinese also employed oars for propelling their ships. Each oar was manned by four crewmen. But sails and oars were not the only methods. They also developed and employed paddlewheel propulsion. The paddlewheel was long considered an invention of the West, but the Chinese were already using it to propel their boats in the fifth century.

By the twelfth century paddlewheel boats were common on China's inland waters. A great many of these were naval vessels. On these craft, paddlewheels were usually arranged in a series on both sides of the hull with a single larger wheel fixed to the stern. Since the steam engine did not exist at the time, the paddlewheels were turned by crewmen inside the hull. They walked endlessly on a series of steps attached to a shaft, turning it and the paddlewheel.

Chinese paddlewheel ships remained in use up to the time of the Opium War of 1839–1842. The Chinese wanted to end trading in opium, but the British wished it to be left alone. The opium trade was enormously lucrative to Western commercial interests. The dispute became overheated, and both sides sought to settle the controversy with guns.

A fleet of Chinese naval paddlewheelers sailed against a squadron of British warships. These had been sent to the Far East to enforce the British government's demands on the Chinese. A spirited engagement took place, and when the smoke cleared, the Chinese ships, sadly outdated and outgunned, had been badly defeated by the more modern and powerful British vessels.

Humanity's climb up the ladder of civilization is marked by definite stages of progress. The primitive Stone Age gradually gave way to a metalworking period. This developed in two distinct stages, the Bronze Age and the Iron Age. Nor were these confined to any one people. Rather, metallurgy sprang up at various times among a number of different groups scattered over the earth.

It is impossible to pinpoint the start of China's

Bronze Age. There is archaeological evidence that Chinese metalworkers knew how to make and cast bronze before 2000 B.C. By 1300 B.C. they were producing bronze castings of very high quality. The study of artifacts discovered by archaeologists strongly suggests that China's Bronze Age began in the valley of the Yellow River, the fertile central part of the country. The region was indeed the cradle of Chinese civilization.

Bronze-making demonstrated to an extraordinary degree the technical skill of the ancient Chinese. Bronze, an alloy of copper and tin (Chinese frequently used lead as well), is a difficult metal to smelt and cast. Yet Chinese metallurgists succeeded in making not only everyday items like pots, bowls, and farming tools, but weapons and intricate artistic pieces as well. Some of the latter included ceremonial vessels and figurines. Few could equal and none surpassed the high artistic merit of the bronzes cast by Chinese metalworkers.

A great many of the artistic bronzes were cast to commemorate some outstanding government or religious event. The occasion was almost always inscribed on the surface of the bronze object. As a result, modern researchers of China's past history have found these bronzes to be valuable sources of information.

The people of the Middle East had known how to make and cast bronze about fifteen hundred years before the Chinese. Historians believe, however, that the process was discovered independently by the Chinese. For their casting method the Chinese first made a solid

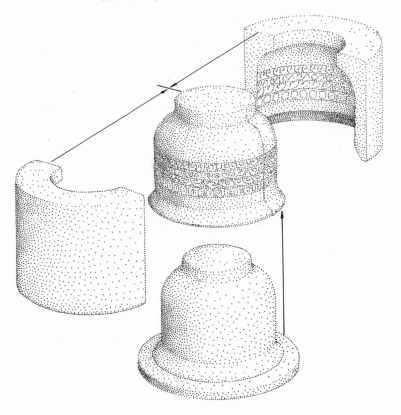

Bronze casting

clay model of the piece to be cast. This became the core after being hardened in a furnace. The core was then covered by another thick coating of clay.

After the outer layer of clay was dry and partly hardened, it was cut into sections and separated from the core. The sections were put into a furnace for additional hardening. The brick-hard sections formed the mold.

To make their casting, Chinese metalworkers reduced the size of the core by cutting away portions of its surface. This formed a space between the core and the mold. Next, the mold sections were fixed firmly around the core. The molten bronze was poured through an opening at the top and filled the space between the core and mold. After the bronze cooled, the mold and core were removed. Finally, high spots on the bronze casting were smoothed away and it was polished.

The less complicated, so-called lost wax method was employed in the West for bronze-casting. This originated in the Middle East as far back as 3500 B.C. The process also included a core, a clay model of the subject to be cast. The core was coated with wax. A layer of clay was placed over the wax. A series of holes punctured this clay coating. The entire piece was baked in a furnace and hardened. The firing also melted the wax, which ran out the holes. After the holes were plugged, molten bronze was poured through a top opening. This flowed into the space formerly filled by the wax. At the end of a cooling period, the mold was broken free and the core removed.

Toward the end of China's Bronze Age, about the fifth century B.C., metalworkers in that country were also using the lost wax method.

In 1980 the people of the United States had an opportunity to see some of the more outstanding bronze objects made by the metalworkers of ancient China. More than one hundred pieces, ceremonial bowls, human and animal figures among others, formed a traveling exhibit, the Great Bronze Age of China, which was shown in five major museums from coast to coast.

The second division of the metalworking period in China, the Iron Age, became increasingly evident by the fifth century B.C. Iron was rapidly displacing bronze for useful things such as farming tools, weapons, and construction material. The Chinese metalworkers were also highly successful at using iron to make a variety of artistic objects.

Just as with bronze, the Chinese were later than some other peoples in working with iron. The Hittites in Asia Minor are considered the first to have learned how to smelt iron ore and cast it, in 1200 B.C. It wasn't until about six hundred years later that Chinese metallurgists found out how to do the same. Nevertheless, this still put them more than a thousand years ahead of the Europeans in the art.

First of the iron-making processes the Chinese learned to perform was the relatively simple method for making wrought iron. This is molten iron that comes from the furnace and cools into a hard, shapeless mass. However, while still glowing red with heat, the iron can be formed, by pounding, into a number of different shapes, an ax, for example, or a hoe.

Chinese iron-makers learned their art quickly and were soon engaged in a more advanced stage of the activity. This was the process for making cast iron, which they were doing on a considerable scale as early as the fourth century B.C. With this technique, the molten iron is guided into molds shaped in the form of the desired object.

The high degree of skill that Chinese iron-makers had acquired enabled them to produce a wide variety of objects, ranging from farming tools and ceremonial bowls to iron roof tiles, statues of Buddha, and animals. Most outstanding of the animal statues was a cast-iron lion twenty feet high, erected in A.D. 954 to commemorate a Chinese victory over the Liao Tartars. But the peak of their iron-casting was reached with the construction of pagodas. A large number of these graceful structures were erected during the Sung Dynasty (A.D. 960–1279).

The great skill the Chinese displayed at smelting and casting iron came to a large extent from their experience in working with bronze. This gave them the know-how to build the proper furnaces for smelting iron ore. Not the least of the necessary features was a refractory material for lining the inner sides of the furnace. It made the furnace able to withstand the high temperatures required to reduce iron ore to a liquid state.

To achieve the necessary high heat in their iron foundries the Chinese metalworkers used coal as a fuel. This was the first instance of the mineral's being employed for generating heat. Coal may have been used as a fuel for smelting iron and other heating purposes two centuries before the Christian era. It was another of the many wonders Marco Polo saw and wrote about. The coal, he said, resembled large black stones and are dug from veins in the mountains. When burned they "flame like logs and consume away like charcoal . . ."

A third process in the ancient Chinese iron industry came into existence with steel-making. This material was created some time in the sixth century A.D., when portions of both wrought iron and cast iron were melted and fused. The resulting product was then subjected to forging, producing a form of surprisingly good steel. Among the first items made from steel were swords.

Pottery-making was another activity common to many peoples of the ancient world. But again, as with bronzes, the potters' skill in China was rarely equaled elsewhere. Pottery ware was carried to new heights by the Chinese with glazes and the production of porcelain. Both of these technical developments are very old. One of the more common beliefs is that they were products of accidental discoveries.

The earliest ceramic glazes appeared during the end of the later Han Dynasty (A.D. 23–220), a period of great technical advancement in China. A crude form of porcelain was also made at this time. However, Chinese potters may have been making an elementary kind of porcelain as early as the ninth century B.C. Pieces of pottery were found by archaeologists dating from that time; when tested, they displayed the characteristics of porcelain.

Porcelain is a relatively thin, hard, and translucent

pottery material. It is made from kaolin, a whitish clay, quartz, and feldspar and is fired in a kiln at very high temperatures. By the sixth and seventh centuries A.D., the time of the T'ang Dynasty, the Chinese were making a white porcelain that was widely admired and remained in demand for decades.

The technique of glazing had also advanced. Chinese potters had learned not only how to produce colored glazes but also how to paint pictorial and other designs beneath the glazes. Besides the T'ang, two other periods in China's history particularly noted for excellent ceramic work were the Sung (960–1279) and the Ming (1368–1644).

In China's ancient times ceramics developed into a widespread industry. Porcelain products in great variety were made — dishes, bowls, vases, and superbly executed figurines. All of these became important in China's trade with her Far Eastern neighbors as well as with countries in the West. Wherever they were introduced, porcelain pieces were received with great admiration. This admiration grew to such a degree that in time porcelain ware and the name China became synonomous. The word "chinaware," or simply "china," was often used in place of "porcelain."

Arab potentates thought that porcelain dishes were so beautiful, they had them embedded in the walls of the rooms of their palaces. European royalty and aristocrats responded in much the same manner in the seventeenth century, when they first saw and felt the beauty of China's porcelain ware. Widely admired,

China's porcelain became an important trade item second only to her silk.

Today, the porcelain pieces made during China's ancient past are still considered superb creations. Major museums throughout the world have acquired extensive collections of porcelain. Private individuals have also assembled many porcelain pieces that in some instances rival museum collections.

Silk was the product made in ancient China that became the country's earliest and most permanent connection with the West. We do not know when this aristocrat of textiles reached the West, but it was long known and widely used in the Middle East by the beginning of the Christian era. Silk was brought to this region via several caravan routes that began in China.

After the Romans added much of the Middle East to their empire, silk became highly popular with them. Wealthy Roman ladies greatly admired the texture and colors of the material for dresswear. Of course, silk was no less desired by the Chinese themselves, as well as their Far Eastern neighbors. The latter even included the warlike tribes of Mongolia. They acquired great quantities of the textile simply by threatening to invade China's northern border. The ruling Chinese emperor at the time would offer rolls of silk in an effort to make them change their minds.

Silk-making is such an old activity in China that there is little more than legend to tell us when or how it began. One tale relates how the wife of the Yellow Emperor was the first to teach the people how to raise silkworms, remove the silk thread from the cocoons, and weave these into a material.

More in line with historical fact, there is evidence that the cultivation of the silkworm (sericulture) and the early development of the silk textile industry were going on as far back as the third millennium B.C. By the late Han Dynasty (A.D. 23–220), it was a large, thriving industry.

The quick and wide acceptance of silk at home and in foreign countries caused the Chinese to realize that they had a valuable product. As a result, they took great pains to keep the complex business of sericulture a secret. Despite their efforts, the information found its way out of China to the West. Once this happened, the monopoly that the Chinese silk manufacturers and merchants enjoyed for centuries was doomed.

Many stories exist that tell how knowledge of silkworm cultivation made its way out of China. One of the more popular comes from the Byzantine writer and government official Procopius. It seems that the Byzantine emperor Justinian was extremely fond of silk. Objecting to the exorbitant prices for the material being charged by Middle Eastern merchants, he decided to establish a silk industry within his empire. A group of Indian monks who had spent many years in China and other regions of the Far East were brought to him one day. The emperor told them what he desired, and they agreed to return to that part of the world and smuggle out the eggs of silkworms. The monks, of course, were to be handsomely rewarded for their dangerous mission.

Reaching the Far East, the monks obtained a supply of silkworm eggs, either in China or in Cambodia, where silkworm cultivation was also carried on. Procopius is not clear on this point. The monks hid the eggs in the hollow of a walking staff and made their way back to Persia, part of the Byzantine Empire in A.D. 552, with the smuggled booty. A year later sericulture was underway in Persia and in Syria, also a Byzantine province.

This tale lacks believability to many authorities because there isn't a word about the vital procedures needed for silkworm cultivation. How sericulture ultimately reached the West still remains a mystery.

As a result of political upheavals in the Middle East, sericulture and the making of silk moved on to Greece. From there the activity eventually entered Sicily, Italy, and Spain.

Cultivating silkworms was, of course, only part of the overall silk industry. After the silkworms were raised and the thread-bearing cocoons obtained, the silk strands had to be removed and made into a fabric. To accomplish this phase of the work Chinese technologists demonstrated a talent for developinig mechanical contrivances that worked successfully. To make silk thread into cloth, it was necessary for the cultivators to produce the first workable textile machinery in the world.

The spinning wheel, silk-winding machines, and water-powered machines for making silk fabric were put together with components that have become basic units in the world of mechanics. Some of these include

A silk-reeling machine

the crank, belt-drive, connecting rod, and piston rod. Although rudimentary at the time, these and other units became essential for the performance of certain mechanical actions, such as converting rotary motion into longitudinal motion. A particularly good example of the skill with which Chinese technologists used mechanical parts was their development of the double-action piston bellows during the second century B.C. By providing a steady flow of air into a blast furnace, the furnace became more efficient for making iron and steel.

A great deal was written about the technical aspects of ancient China's textile industry. One of the best accounts, the *Ts'an Shu*, was written by Ch'in Kuan in A.D. 1090. He gives a detailed description of the important silk-winding machine. It is noteworthy that all these contrivances were fully operational in the eleventh and twelfth centuries, several hundred years before similar mechanical parts and machines were known to Europeans.

When the age of invention came to Europe the machinery it produced turned that continent's social and economic order upside down. Historians have labeled the era the Industrial Revolution. The machines basic to its success, particularly the steam engine, were largely put together with mechanical components that had long been used by Chinese technologists.

After Europe became the center of technical activity, beginning about the seventeenth century, the accomplishments of technologists there were truly of remarkable dimensions. And in the history of technology, they have been properly recognized as such. However, in the same history there is little that acknowledges the equally impressive achievements of Chinese technologists working centuries earlier. Only now are scholars beginning to appreciate what these inventors really accomplished and are rightfully enlarging their share of deserved recognition.

6. Engineering in Ancient China

The Great Wall of China is one of the engineering marvels of the ancient world. Even in our modern age of technological and engineering wonders, the Wall arouses admiration for the skill of the builders of the past. Comparable in magnitude in conception and construction to the Pyramids of Egypt, the Great Wall has been a world-renowned attraction for tourists through the ages.

In ancient times China was torn by seemingly endless wars. There were civil wars among rulers of the various kingdoms contending for supremacy. Wars were fought against invasions by outside enemy forces. As a means of protection in all of these conflicts the Chinese turned to the construction of walls.

Walls were erected around homes; they encircled the grounds of the emperor's palace; walls were even built around cities and along the frontiers of provinces. But the greatest of these by far was the Great Wall, stretching hundreds of miles along China's northern boundary. It was put up to keep out the warrior tribes of Mongolia, who were forever invading China's northern provinces.

The great Wall came into existence in piecemeal fashion. Sections of the Wall were built at various times, and these eventually were connected to form the entire Great Wall. China's first emperor, Ch'in Shih Huang Ti, in 221 B.C. began the work of joining into a continuous barrier the separate walls that had been erected by the rulers of the northern kingdoms.

Emperor Ch'in had conquered all the independent kingdoms between China's northern Mongolian frontier and the Yangtze River. His chief concern after unifying China was not the danger of rebellion within his realm but the nomadic tribes on his northern frontier. Consequently, he believed a wall along that perimeter would do much to reduce the problem. In addition, such a wall would make it unnecessary to maintain a huge defensive army, thus eliminating a drain on the treasury. The wily emperor had yet another reason for constructing the Great Wall. The enormous task would keep his soldiers occupied and their minds off schemes to undermine the emperor's rule.

The gigantic construction project was given to one of the emperor's most capable generals, Mêng T'ien, who was also a first-rate engineer. Thousands of soldiers and civilians labored under the harshest conditions, including beatings and death, to complete the Wall.

The Great Wall's eastern terminus was the town of

Shan-hai Kuan on the shore of the Gulf of Chihli, a northern extension of the Yellow Sea. Making its way westward, the Great Wall soared in sweeping curves up mountainsides, then down into deep valleys, to end more than two thousand miles away in the desert wastelands of the northwest Province of Kansu. If all the branches of the Great Wall were to be included, the monster barrier would have a length of over three thousand miles.

The Great Wall was constructed basically of tamped earth and stone, the center or core of the barrier. This was covered with several layers of bricks or granite blocks. The latter material depended on its availability in the region where the Wall was being built. If present, granite was quarried and used. Otherwise, bricks were substituted.

The base of the Wall ranged from twenty-five to thirty feet in width. Its height averaged thirty feet. The top of the Wall formed a causeway ten to twelve feet wide. The Wall's sloping sides ended in a low parapet bordering the causeway. The parapet had openings at regular intervals through which defending troops shot their crossbows.

Watchtowers, one or two stories high, were erected along the causeway every two hundred yards. A parapet crowned each tower, giving the Wall's defenders an excellent observation point. There were eight to twelve watchtowers in every mile of the Wall's length.

The towers were positioned for the best possible military advantage. Some were at the top of mountains;

The Great Wall

some at the edge of steep ravines. They were also just far enough apart so that the arrows shot by the cross-bowmen would cover the space between. Soldiers manning the watchtowers communicated with smoke signals.

The Great Wall did not bar the peaceful north-south movement of people. At those points where the Wall crossed major travel routes, sturdy gates provided openings for passage.

Scouring winds, storms, and the stone-cracking cold of winter have taken their toll of the Great Wall. Neglect also played a large part in the Wall's eventual disintegration, even though attempts at repairing it were made from time to time. These efforts usually depended on the political situation existing between China and her northern Mongolian neighbors.

One of the last large-scale programs to restore the Great Wall to its original condition took place during the Ming Dynasty in the fourteenth century. This was a period shortly after the Chinese had driven the last of the Mongols from their land. The Mongols had breached the Great Wall and subjugated the Chinese for more than a century. But even the Ming restoration crumbled in time, and the Great Wall that present-day tourists come to see is a twentieth-century reconstruction.

The Chinese civilization began its development on the fertile alluvial plains bordering the Yellow and Yangtze Rivers. Both of these great waterways and their many tributaries played vital roles in the lives of the ancient Chinese. The rivers were both constructive and destructive. They nourished crops planted in the rich soil; they became convenient avenues of transportation; but they were also cruel when their waters rushed over the banks to ravage the countryside.

The rivers were ever-present in the lives of the Chinese. In the past, as now, hydraulic engineers worked ceaselessly to tame the power of these waterways and to make them contribute greater benefits to the people. Centuries before the Christian era, Chinese engineers undertook hydraulic projects remarkable in nature and scope. Dikes, vast irrigation systems, and canals were constructed, a number of which continue to be useful to this day.

An extensive irrigation system was laid out with great skill on the plains bordering the Yangtze River in the fifth century B.C. Thereafter it was constantly maintained, improved, and enlarged. In A.D. 321 two giant reservoirs were constructed near the modern city of Chinkiang in Kiangsu Province. These assured water for the irrigation ditches during times of drought, when the Yangtze fell far below its normal level.

Central China's many lakes and winding river tributaries were made use of by the people as travel routes very early in that country's history. In the beginning, these waterways were adequate for the needs of the people. But as time passed and China's population increased, new cities were established, and farming and commerce expanded. The need for a better system of water transportation became evident. One answer, as the hydraulic engineers saw it, would be the construction of canals to connect the separated natural waterways. This would result in a greatly extended water transportation network serving vast new areas of the country as well as newly created cities.

The emperors who ruled China over the many centuries for the most part gave the engineers enthusiastic support for the canal-building projects. They were convinced the canals would be of both economic benefit and military value. Troops and supplies could be moved to troubled areas a good deal more conveniently than previously.

Some of the earliest of the major canal-construction projects took place during the time China was divided into the Three Kingdoms (A.D. 220–280). Six long stretches of canals were built in the Wei Kingdom in the north and northwest parts of China. Some were also constructed in the south of China, the Kingdom of Wu.

However, it wasn't until China became reunified under the Sui (A.D. 590–618) that engineers launched canal-building projects in a big way. The work continued for almost three centuries. Separate stretches of the older canals between the Yangtze and Yellow Rivers had fallen into disrepair and needed rebuilding. New canals were constructed so that by 618 a water-transportation network covered a huge inland region of China, in a north-south direction as well as east and west. Some of the earliest stretches of what was to be the supreme achievement of the hydraulic engineers, the Grand Canal, were built during this period.

The canals of ancient China were not simple ditches flooded with water. They were well planned and constructed, combining usefulness and attractiveness. A writer of the period has given us a description of a typical canal. On the average the navigable waterway was about forty paces wide. Roads extended along both banks. Elms and willow trees were planted along the water's edge and in many places formed a green arch over the canals. Pleasant routes such as this ran for hundreds of miles through the countryside. Rest stations were built along the canals' embankments at regular intervals. These permitted the crews of the sampans and small junks to tie up their craft and go ashore to refresh themselves. Between these stations were others that were more elaborate; they were built especially for the emperor when he traveled along the canals.

Though these canals were extremely useful to China for many centuries, they were built at a great cost in human suffering. Historical accounts of their construction reveal that five and a half million people were impressed by the government to dig and haul away the soil. In some regions where canal construction took place, every male from fifteen to fifty-five years of age was forced to join labor gangs. Some fifty thousand overseers saw to it that there were no idle shovels or wheelbarrows. The laggards were dealt with in the harshest manner — whipped or made to carry cumbersome neck weights. Defiant loafers were taken care of permanently. Their heads were chopped off.

To help keep this huge army of workers fed, every

fifth family in villages close to canal construction was required to prepare and bring food to the laborers. Children, old men, and women were involved with this assignment. It has been estimated that China's network of canals cost the lives of close to two million individuals.

The Grand Canal, greatest of China's ancient canal-building accomplishments, ranks with the Great Wall as one of China's engineering triumphs. Like the Great Wall the canal was made up of separate sections built at different times. Some of the individual stretches dated back to the fourth century B.C. One of the oldest of these was the Pien Ch'u Canal, connecting the Yellow River with the Huai Valley.

In its original full length the Grand Canal extended roughly in a north-south direction from the capital city of Loyang in the north to the lower Yangtze Valley in the south. During the thirteenth century, when China was under the rule of Mongol Yuan emperors, the canal was rebuilt and made longer. It ran from Peking in the north to Hangchow in the south for a distance of about eleven hundred miles, about as far as from New York to Florida. By connecting the Yangtze and Yellow Rivers, the Grand Canal provided a valuable inland transportation route for farm products and manufactured goods.

The most difficult problem that engineers building the Grand Canal had to face was a high point near the Shantung Mountains. The water had to be made to rise 138 feet above sea level and the canal kept at full depth so that canal boats could navigate. Engineers overcame a good part of the difficulty by building a giant reservoir. The impounded waters flooded the canal stretch to a proper level.

When Westerners began to visit China in the thirteenth century, they were greatly impressed by many sights. China's extensive system of canals was not the least of these. After returning to Italy and writing about wonders he had seen during his long visit to China, Marco Polo mentioned canals as having excited his special admiration. "The Great Khan has made very great channels both broad and deep from one river to the other and from one lake to the other; and makes the water go through the channels so that they seem a great river: and quite large ships go through with grain."

In the course of building canals, dikes, and other water projects, Chinese hydraulic engineers pioneered in the use of lock gates for canal shipping and the caisson. The latter is a watertight compartment that permits underwater workers to perform their tasks. In modern times the caisson was improved over the early Chinese version, providing vital equipment in the construction of bridge towers and tunnels, among other hydraulic engineering projects.

Chinese hydraulic engineers of ancient times were among the greatest in the world. All who saw the skillful construction of their projects had only words of praise. But there was something else about their dikes, irrigation systems, and canals: they had a remarkably enduring quality. Even after many centuries, much of what they created is still proving useful.

The mountains and valleys of western China, and the numerous waterways in the central part of the country, made bridge construction a necessity on the main travel routes. Chinese engineers designed several different kinds of bridges to suit particular situations. The suspension bridge was frequently employed for spanning deep valleys in mountainous regions.

The suspension bridge was made of bamboo cables strung from one side of a valley or riverbank to the other. The cables supported a walkway that hung by a series of vertical lines. The cables were made from long strips of bamboo twisted to form a strong, single line.

But the bamboo cables had their limits of endurance. There were many occasions when they snapped and catapulted travelers to their death below. Thus, when iron-making became common in China, bridge engineers quickly substituted iron chains for bamboo. The first bridge using iron-chain cables was erected in the seventh century A.D., during the Sui Dynasty. This was a period when China witnessed a great deal of technical activity and achieved many firsts. The iron-chain suspension bridge proved highly successful, and a number of them were built during the later Sung, Tuan, and Ming Dynasties. As happened with so many technological developments in ancient times, Chinese bridge-builders, with their use of iron, were centuries ahead of their European counterparts. It wasn't until 1741 that European engineers first employed iron in bridge construction.

The Chinese pioneered another type of bridge in which iron was also used. This was the segmental arch bridge. The structure was the brain child of a noted engineer, Li Ch'un. He built the graceful bridge in A.D. 610 at Chao-Hsien, Hopei Province. The bridge was constructed with a long center arch and a series of smaller supporting arches at the spandrel ends. Iron clamps were used to help hold the stones in place in the smaller arches. Repaired a number of times over the centuries, this historic bridge is still in use. The famous Ponte Vecchio, built in 1345 in Florence, Italy,

Segmented arch bridge at Chao-Hsien, built in A.D. 610

was the first segmental arch bridge to be constructed in Europe.

The subject of petroleum is one of paramount interest in many parts of the world. This is especially true in the industrialized nations of the West, whose economic existence is largely dependent on the liquid mineral. In an effort to find new oil deposits, wide-ranging drilling operations are being carried out as never before.

The drilling methods employed today are much advanced over those used at the turn of the century, when the industry was in its infancy. Those early drilling techniques to a great degree were first developed and used by the Chinese nearly two centuries before the Christian era. They had learned ways of drilling holes as much as two thousand feet deep to obtain brine and natural gas. Both substances existed in large underground deposits in the central province of Szechuan.

The main tools used by the Chinese drillers were long bamboo poles tipped with steel cutting points. A group of workers would jump on and off a wooden beam, arranged seesaw fashion, to create a rocking motion. The power produced was guided to a mechanical hook-up for driving the bamboo drill into the earth. As this action was taking place, other workers hauled back and forth on a rope twined around the drill to rotate it. Since bamboo is hollow, forming a natural pipe, it also was used to bring the brine and gas to the surface. This method of deep drilling may have been first used in Europe in the twelfth century for artesian wells.

In modern times, one result of the reliance on oil has been a growing interest in alternate sources of power, such as solar energy. Buildings and private homes are being designed, constructed, and positioned to take advantage of the sun's heating power. This is not a modern development. Chinese engineers were doing this centuries ago. They were not only careful about the placement of buildings for catching the maximum heat from the sun; they laid out entire cities with that renewable energy source in mind.

The Westward Travels of Ancient Chinese Science and Technology

How did the ancient Chinese achievements in science and technology eventually reach the West? This is a question that has long puzzled historians. Little factual evidence exists, and what is available is often unclear. Scholars have thus had to resort to theories, which one may accept or argue with at will.

There is one point, however, that almost all are in agreement with — and that is the element of time. The westward movement was not a short-term affair. It was a long, slow process spanning more than twenty centuries. Yet by the time Europe had emerged from the so-called Dark Ages, many of China's scientific and technological accomplishments had already reached the West. In the opinion of some historians specializing in that phase of China's past, these scientific and technical triumphs contributed a good deal to the advancement of civilization in the Western world.

Because of virtually nonexisting communications in ancient times, peoples of the Western and Eastern worlds were almost totally unknown to each other. Western scholars could write little about the Chinese civilization or the immense land mass between the East and the West. One of the few who tried was Ptolemy, the Greek-Egyptian astronomer and geographer of the second century A.D.

Ptolemy included bits of information about the vast region between the Middle East and China in his geographical writings. Much of what he recorded was surprisingly accurate. He had obtained his information from traders traveling with caravans. By Ptolemy's time a number of trade routes stretching from the Mediterranean world to the Far East had become established.

The most famous and heavily traveled trade route between China and the West was the Old Silk Road. Much of its length had been pioneered by Chang Ch'ien, an emissary sent west by the Emperor Han Wu Ti (140–87 B.C.). Chang's mission was to establish friendly relations with the independent rulers of lands beyond China's western frontier. Many rolls of silk were among his tokens of friendship. The ambassador thus helped to create a demand for this beautiful Chinese fabric.

Chang traveled as far west as Bactria, part of which is now Afghanistan. At the time of Chang's arrival, Bactria was under the control of the Romans. Following the ambassador's return to China after an absence of eleven years, the route Chang blazed became a well-traveled road of commerce. Silk was the most common and valuable product borne over the road, eventually giving it the name by which it was best known. The first west-bound caravan over the Old Silk Road left China some time in 106 B.C.

The Old Silk Road was no easy route. It rose cork-screw fashion to the dizzying heights of mountains, skirted the edges of deep valleys, and crossed miles of parched desert. The road began in two places in central China — Loyang and Changan. Both were capital cities of the early and late Han Dynasties. Changan, western-most of the two cities, was the more popular starting point. It was a cosmopolitan city bustling with the activities of traders, many of whom were from Persia, Syria, and Arabia.

Caravans left China proper through the Jade Gate, westernmost opening through the Great Wall. After weeks of weary traveling the caravan finally arrived in Baghdad, Persia, known today as Iran. Some traders in the caravan would continue on to marketplaces in Syria and Lebanon. By the time the caravan reached the western ends of the Old Silk Road, it was no longer its original starting size. A number of traders would prefer to carry on their business in such cities as Kash-bar, Bokhara, and Samarkand, scattered along the road. They returned to China by joining other caravans that had started in the West.

Travelers along the Old Silk Road had to face not

only natural dangers but man-made hazards as well. Bandits were a constant annoyance. So too were petty rulers through whose lands the caravans passed and who demanded tribute for the privilege. As protection against banditry and the unreasonable demands of tribal chiefs, large numbers of soldiers generally accompanied a caravan.

Because of the riches to be had in the West, caravans were extremely large. And they were not always composed entirely of traders and their guards. Government officials and their aides, acrobatic troupes, pilgrims heading for distant shrines, and just plain adventurers were also among the travelers. Carts filled with rolls of silk, pottery ware, carved ivory, and other merchandise were pulled by oxen. Camels with huge bundles fixed to their backs and horses and donkeys made up the varied means of transport. Many individuals, of course, simply followed along on foot.

At the numerous encampments, villages, and cities en route, there was frequent contact between the travelers and the natives through whose lands they were passing. This produced an exchange of information and ideas. It is believed that this was one of the important ways that Chinese achievements in science and their many inventions moved westward. This did not take place in one giant leap but in stages over an extremely long period.

The Old Silk Road was not a one-way avenue of commerce or of ideas from China to the West. There was also a movement of both from west to east. Merchants heading for China bore such products as glass-ware, amber, incense, purple dye, and woolen material. Many natural products also moved in both directions along the road. The West sent to China such plants as the grapevine, alfalfa, cucumber, fig, sesame, and the walnut tree. In return, the West was introduced to the orange, peach, pear, and such popular Chinese garden plants as the rose, peony, azalea, and chrysanthemum.

For a millennium the Old Silk Road continued as an active, important communications link between the East and the West. Then it experienced a period of decline, brought on in part by intensified banditry. There was a second phase of great popularity during the time of the Mongol Empire in the twelfth and thirteenth centuries. After the collapse of the empire in the late fourteenth century, and the restoration of China's independence, the Old Silk Road came to the end of its role as a major route of communications between China and the West.

Although the land connection had lost its significance, it did not mean that there was no longer contact between the peoples of the two widely separated worlds. A sea link that had been established far to the south of the Old Silk Road had become increasingly important.

The Greeks, Egyptians, and the Romans were among the earliest to pioneer the western reaches of this sea route. Some two hundred years before Christianity they were sailing their lumbering craft down the Red Sea and Persian Gulf as far east as India and beyond.

There is some evidence that after the third century A.D. they were regularly visiting along China's southeast coast.

It remained for the Arabs, however, to become the chief developers of the sea lanes to China. Following the establishment of the Islamic religion by Muhammad in the seventh century, his legions, trumpeting the beliefs of the Prophet, stormed to power throughout the Middle East and to the western borders of China. Turning to the West, they conquered all of northern Africa as well as a large portion of southern Europe. In the eighth century their empire included control of the seas south of the Arabian Peninsula and as far east as India.

As the Arabs guided their cargo ships farther eastward, they eventually reached China. Aggressive merchants, the Arabs and Chinese were soon engaged in a brisk trade. This continued at an ever-increasing pace throughout the eighth and ninth centuries. The Arabs thought so highly of the Chinese market that they established colonies in Canton and Hangchow. The main articles of trade between the two peoples were silk, pottery ware, and carved ivory from China and spices from the Arabian Peninsula.

Chinese mariners, meantime, were almost as busy developing the eastern portion of the east-west sea connection. They were sailing their junks westward to India and beyond. By the end of the twelfth century the Chinese had displaced the Arabs as the chief carriers along the entire route.

The sea link between China and the West was as active for the interchange of commerce and ideas as the Old Silk Road. It is almost a certainty to many historians that the Chinese invention of the compass became known to the West via this sea route. Perhaps in the same way the West was introduced to the unique ship-construction features developed by the Chinese — hull compartments and sternpost rudder, among others.

There were other items that moved along the east-west sea connection, like tea. Information about this herb was brought to the West by the Arabs in the middle of the ninth century. Southern Chinese had been drinking tea in the first century of the Christian era; perhaps earlier. After Europeans found out about tea's stimulating quality they gradually came to enjoy it in the 1600s. Playing cards were still another item made known to the West by Arabs traveling the sea lanes to China. Unlike tea, which took some time to catch on, playing cards were accepted almost immediately by Europeans.

The third, but no less important, link of communication between the West and China was the arrival of Catholic missionaries during the late sixteenth and early seventeenth centuries. This connection differed from those described above in that the flow of information or knowledge was mainly from west to east.

The arrival of the missionaries, mostly Jesuits, was an event of some significance. Chinese emperors, since the overthrow and expulsion of the Mongols in the fourteenth century, had placed a tight ban on outsiders coming into their country and on Chinese going out. Father Matteo Ricci and several Jesuit colleagues were the first arrivals from the West to enter China under a relaxation of that ban. The Italian missionaries arrived in Peking in 1601 from Macao, an island off the southeast China coast. The missionaries had been brought to this island by the Portuguese in 1562. Macao had been taken possession of by Portugal and still remains under its rule.

Father Matteo Ricci, an extraordinary man, left a lasting impression on Chinese scholars. He was a great intellectual, a scholar of wide interests, and a born linguist. After only a short time among the natives, he was able to read, write, and speak Chinese with remarkable fluency.

Jesuits undergo a long and rigorous training, not only in theology but also in such secular subjects as philosophy, history, and science. Some of the leading scientists of Renaissance Europe had taught Father Ricci. By the time the missionary left for the Far East he had been well schooled in mathematics, astronomy, cosmology, and geography. The Jesuit missionary had brought the highest intellectual attainments of the Renaissance to China. Along with his Jesuit colleagues Father Ricci expounded on Western philosophy, mathematics, astronomy, and geography. One of Father Ricci's more noteworthy contributions was his drawing of a map of the world as it was presumed to be in the sixteenth century. It was so highly thought of by Chinese scholars that copies were printed and circulated throughout China.

Father Ricci continued to add to his esteem among Chinese scholars by collaborating with several of them in translating leading European books on astronomy, mathematics, hydraulics, and, of course, religion. Death in 1610 put an end to the efforts of this learned man to bring the widely separated worlds of the West and East closer together.

The prime reason Father Ricci and his colleagues made such a deep impression on China's intellectuals was that the West, by the sixteenth century, had begun to play a leading role in scholarly attainments. The Chinese were no longer making original contributions in such fields as astronomy, mathematics, or technology, as they had in earlier times. Thus, they welcomed the opportunity given by the Jesuits to catch up with the latest achievements of Western scholars in many of those areas.

A comparable situation exists today in that Western scientific and technical knowledge is once again flowing into China on a considerable scale. For decades the country was torn by internal strife and external wars, which produced chaos and stagnation in all fields of endeavor. While the West moved far ahead in science and technology, the Chinese came to a virtual standstill.

United now under a new government system, communism, the People's Republic of China is experiencing a period of relative calm and progress. With these conditions prevailing, government officials, scholars, and engineers are attempting to adapt the most advanced scientific and technological triumphs of the

West to China's special needs. In a sense, this may be considered an appropriate historical exchange for all the scientific and technical achievements that China passed along to the West in ancient times. With the help of the West, and in view of the intelligence and ingenuity of her people, China may well achieve once again her past glories in science and technology.

Major Dynasties

	B.C.
Hsia Dynasty	ca. 2205–ca. 1766
(*Uncertain — no clear evidence of its existence.*)	
Shang Dynasty	ca. 1766?–ca. 1122?
Chou Dynasty	ca. 1122?–ca. 256?
Ch'in Dynasty	221–207
Former or Western Han Dynasty	202–A.D. 9

	A.D.
Hsin Dynasty	9–23
Later Han Dynasty	25–220
Three Kingdoms	220–280
(*Wei, North; Shu, West; Wu, South*)	
Western Chin Dynasty	266–316
(*From 316 to 581 China was divided and ruled by various kingdoms. These were distributed in northern and southern halves of China.*)	

Sui Dynasty	590–618
(*Ruled unified China.*)	
T'ang Dynasty	618–906
(*From 907 to 960 China was again broken up and ruled briefly by Five Dynasties [North] and Ten Kingdoms [South].*)	
Sung Dynasty	960–1279
Yuan Dynasty	1279–1368
(*Mongols*)	
Ming Dynasty	1368–1644
Ch'ing Dynasty	1644–1912
(*Manchus*)	
Republic of China	1912–1949
People's Republic of China	1949–
(*Communist Rule*)	

* Based mainly on "China's Imperial Past" by Charles O. Hucker

Additional Reading

Breur, Hans. *Columbus Was Chinese: Discoveries and Inventions of the Far East.* New York: Herder & Herder, 1972.

Carter, T. F. *The Invention of Printing in China and Its Spread Westward.* New York: Columbia University Press, 1925; rev. ed., 1931 and 1955.

Dawson, Raymond, ed. *The Legacy of China.* New York: Oxford University Press, paperback, 1964.

Donnelly, I. A. *Chinese Junks: A Book of Drawings in Black and White.* Shanghai: Kelley & Walsh, 1924.

Gilbert, K. S., ed. *Treasures from the Bronze Age of China.* Collection of Metropolitan Museum of Art. New York: Ballantine Books, 1980.

Goodrich, L. Carrington. *A Short History of the Chinese People.* New York: Harper & Row, paperback, 1959.

Hart, Clive. *Kites: An Historical Survey.* New York: Frederick A. Praeger, 1967.

Hodges, Henry. *Technology in the Ancient World.* New York: Alfred A. Knopf, 1970.

Hommel, Rudolph P. *China at Work,* Cambridge, Mass.: The MIT Press, 1937.

Hucker, Charles O. *China's Imperial Past.* Stanford: Stanford University Press, 1975.

Lum, Peter. *The Growth of Civilization in East Asia.* New York: S. G. Phillips, 1969.

Majno, Guido. *The Healing Hand: Man and Wound in the Ancient World.* Cambridge, Mass.: Harvard University Press, 1975.

Needham, Joseph. *Science and Civilisation in China.* Vol. I, 1954; Vol. II, 1956; Vol. III, 1959; Vol. IV, Part 1, 1962; Vol. IV, Part 2, 1965; Vol. IV, Part 3, 1971. Cambridge: Cambridge University Press.

Palo, Dr. Stephan. *The Chinese Art of Healing.* New York: Herder & Herder, 1972.

Partington, J. R. *A History of Greek Fire and Gunpowder.* Cambridge: W. Herfer & Sons Ltd., 1960.

Ronan, Colin A. *The Shorter Science and Civilization in China,* Vol. 1. Cambridge: Cambridge University Press, 1978.

Severin, Timothy. *The Oriental Adventure: Explorers of the East.* Boston: Little, Brown & Co., 1976.

Thorwald, Jürgen, *Science and Secrets of Early Medicine.* New York: Harcourt, Brace & World, Inc., 1963.

Usher, Abbott Payson. *A History of Mechanical Inventions.* Cambridge, Mass.: Harvard University Press, 1954.

Index